Super-Productive

Super-Productive

120 STRATEGIES TO DO MORE AND STRESS LESS

Sharon F. Danzger

ISBN: 0692834281
ISBN 13: 9780692834282
Library of Congress Control Number: 2017900662
Lane 5 Press, New York, NY

*In loving memory of
my super-productive parents,
Lenore and George Feldman*

Contents

Acknowledgments

My heartfelt thanks to my husband, Neil, and kids Ben, Adam, Dan, and Georgia, for supporting me throughout the process of writing and publishing this book.

To my husband and brothers David, Andrew, and Michael Feldman, who proofread and encouraged me, especially when I was filled with self-doubt, thank you! Mom and Dad were right—they would not always be here, but we are truly blessed to have each other.

I am so appreciative of the many residential and corporate clients I have engaged with over the years. Working with you has enabled me to grow and develop as a trainer and coach. Your challenges became my challenges and your successes continue to bring me great personal satisfaction.

Finally, I am grateful to my parents, of blessed memory, who were fantastic role models for me and my brothers. They showed us how to be super-productive while flourishing and living a life of meaning.

Introduction

I am fortunate that I was born with the genetic disposition to be very organized. I was unaware that this was a unique skill until I was almost forty years old, and my mother suggested I start a business as a professional organizer. I was surprised (and thrilled) to realize that people would actually pay me to help them with something that I am good at and love doing.

I began researching: I spoke with other professional organizers (special thanks to Marcie Singer, who answered my many questions and gave me insight into what it takes to successfully help others), attended a NAPO (National Association of Professional Organizers) conference in Boston, and read many, many books on organizing.

When I felt ready to give it a go, I reached out to family and friends to test my skills on them. After about a dozen positive experiences, I began marketing my services as a professional organizer in 2006.

Over the years, I have worked with many individuals to help them declutter their homes, create organizational systems, and improve time management. I also helped with estate cleanouts to maximize the economics of a home when someone passed away. But the area of my business I found most thrilling was speaking to groups of people, offering strategies that could help them get more done without feeling overwhelmed and stressed.

At the end of 2013, I decided to focus on my greatest strengths and went all in on redirecting my business toward corporate training and individual coaching related to personal productivity.

I am often asked how I get so much done—building my own business, raising four kids, swimming, volunteering, pursuing my passion for learning new things, and playing video games. Yes—I am a big fan of Facebook's one-minute video game *Bejeweled Blitz!*

The truth is, while I was blessed with some innate organizational skills, I am not extraordinary in terms of what I accomplish. I simply have good systems and routines in place. And so can you.

I have spent a lot of time breaking down and analyzing the concept of time management. What gets in the way of people having the time to do the things about which they are passionate? Why does life feel so hard at times? How come everyone is so busy doing things they don't care about?

More importantly, I wanted to identify small changes *anyone* can make that will give life greater meaning while reducing stress.

The overwhelming majority of my clients and trainees are smart and successful. They have attended premier universities and work for top-rated firms in a variety of industries, from big banks to midsize financial service firms, pharmaceutical companies, universities, and nonprofits.

Very often, it only takes small tweaks in daily routines, paying attention to some subconscious behaviors, and making a little effort to gain greater control of your time. By approaching your work more proactively, you can trigger a tremendous increase in productivity.

When we get better quality work done in less time, it frees us up to enjoy other aspects of our lives—family, friends, and hobbies.

This book is designed to offer practical strategies that can be incorporated into your life with minimal effort for maximum impact.

I suggest focusing on the concepts that seem so easy you can't believe you haven't been doing them all along.

If you come across an idea that you've heard of or thought about doing before…ignore it. You might have the best intentions, but if it was too cumbersome to do it the first time, you're not likely to follow through with it this time either. With 120 strategies, why make it hard for yourself? Start with what seems easy and natural.

You're better off finding a strategy you are sure you can succeed at and implement.

Being productive with less stress shouldn't be hard! But it also doesn't happen overnight.

Start with one or two things. Practice your new skill or habit daily until it is part of your routine. Think of each new habit as a twenty-one-day challenge.

You will read later in the book about the theory that it takes twenty-one days to change a habit. Once you no longer have to think about it, add something new. If you create a new habit each month, you will have made twelve positive habit changes in a year!

Building on small successes will boost your confidence and make you realize that this is all within your reach.

When you try to change everything at once, you are likely to fail, which will make you feel worse when it's simply that you expected too much of yourself in the first place.

As you do have successes, I would love to hear about them. You can find me on LinkedIn, Facebook, Twitter, and Instagram. And you can always e-mail me at Sharon@ControlChaos.org.

CHAPTER 1

E-Mails

Technology is a useful servant but a dangerous master.
—CHRISTIAN LOUS LANGE

When I begin a training session, I like to ask, "What gets in the way of you being your most productive?" E-mail is always at the top of the list. It seems to be a pervasive issue that cuts across industry and level. So I thought we should tackle it first!

1. Unsubscribe

One of the easiest ways to reduce the volume of e-mail in your inbox is to unsubscribe from mailing lists. Remember that every time you order something online, they will automatically add you back to their list.

There are a few ways to get off a mailing list. The simplest is to scroll down to the bottom of the e-mail and click unsubscribe. The type is often very small and the link hard to find...but it's there.

There are also services like Unroll.me (https://unroll.me) and SaneBox (https://www.sanebox.com) that can make the process go much faster. Unroll.me lists all of your subscriptions and makes it very easy to select Keep in Inbox, Roll Up, or Unsubscribe. The Roll Up items appear in a digest—so it's one e-mail in your inbox and you can scan its contents to make sure you don't miss an important offer or sale at a favorite retailer.

If you are looking for more sophisticated help with your e-mail, I suggest looking into SaneBox. This service uses algorithms to anticipate how your e-mails should be handled based on your actions. It tracks your behavior and makes adjustments so it becomes increasingly accurate over time.

2. Limit e-mail review

You are probably checking e-mail too often.

Michelle Klein is Head of Marketing for North America at Facebook. According to her presentation in May of 2016 at Social Media Week in NYC, adults check their phone 30 times a day on average and millennials check their phone more than 150 times a day. While checking is not specific to e-mail (it might also be to check the calendar; look at an app; or surf Facebook, Twitter, Instagram, and other social-media sites), it is certainly a distraction to getting work done.

A study done at the University of British Columbia tested the connection between e-mail and stress. They instructed one group of participants to check e-mail as often as they'd like, keeping their e-mail application open and notifications (those pop-ups that appear and fade to indicate the arrival of a new e-mail) on. The other group was told to limit checking e-mails to three times a day. When they were not reviewing e-mails, their e-mail application needed to stay closed and the notifications turned off.

Both groups' cortisol levels (an indicator of stress) were checked throughout and the time it took to process e-mail each day was measured and recorded. At the end of the week, the two groups switched parameters so that both groups were tested under both scenarios.

The results? The group that checked more frequently had significantly higher cortisol (stress) levels. And, although the other group was not able to cut back to three times a day and crept up to checking five times a day, on average, the time it took them to process their e-mails was still 20 percent less.

If you are looking for ways to get time back each week, think about this: For an average forty-hour workweek, you could be saving two hours simply by checking e-mail less. A McKinsey study estimates that you spend 28 percent of your day on e-mail. If you round this to 25 percent, this means you spend ten hours a week on e-mail. Saving 20 percent of this time gives you two hours back a week.

Many clients have expressed concern over checking e-mail infrequently. They argue that it simply would not be accepted in their work environment. Knowing how many law firms and investment banks operate, I believe this is true. However, if it's considered acceptable to be in a meeting for an hour without checking e-mail, the door is open.

Consider having a conversation with your boss, explaining that in order to do your best work in the least amount of time, you will sometimes need to check e-mail less frequently (say hourly, instead of every five minutes.) Perhaps you can come up with a way for you to be reached (outside of e-mail) should an emergency arise. It could be coming by your desk in person, texting, or calling on the phone.

We sometimes forget that e-mail is only one of many ways to communicate. Even e-mail provides opportunities for filtering to allow your VIP senders to chime through when others cannot.

3. Process efficiently

Now that you know to check e-mail less often, you are probably wondering how to do it most efficiently. I recommend the following system, based on Michael Linenberger's *Total Workday Control Using Microsoft Outlook.*

- The four *D*s
  Start by **DELETING** unwanted e-mails.
  DO anything that takes less than two minutes.
  DELEGATE work that needs to be done by another by forwarding the e-mail to them.
  DEFER more thoughtful replies that require some time by adding the task to your to-do list.

- Inbox Zero:
  This is by no means a must, but if you are interested in achieving Inbox Zero (an empty e-mail inbox), you can. Once you have processed e-mails and added the tasks required by them to your to-do list, put all the e-mails into a Processed E-mail Folder. This will enable you to search them, if needed, while uncluttering your Inbox.

- E-mail filing:
  If you are uncomfortable grouping all e-mails in a processed e-mail folder, create an e-mail filing system that is similar to your paper filing system. Once you have processed e-mails and added the tasks required by them to your to-do list, file e-mails in their appropriate folders. Doing this every time you review e-mails will keep your inbox empty.

4. Be concise

> *Brevity is the soul of the wit.*
> —WILLIAM SHAKESPEARE

When you scan through your e-mails, which do you read first—the long ones or the short ones? I'm guessing you read the short ones first; after all, it's much easier to knock them off.

Make it easy for your audience by getting right to the heart of the matter. Save the flowery descriptions for your first novel.

E-mails should be direct and to the point. Some say e-mails should be no more than three sentences. I'll let you determine the best length, but remember—less is more.

5. Use the subject line

One of the easiest ways to get your e-mail read is by using your subject line effectively. Letting your audience know the content and urgency of your e-mail enables them to act accordingly.

It is especially useful in prioritizing what to open and read first. My five favorite subject line abbreviations are:

- FYI = For Your Information
- NRN = No Reply Needed
- AR = Action Required
- EOM = End of Message
- RB = Reply By

It is important to inform colleagues when you begin using subject-line abbreviations. Otherwise, it can backfire on you and create confusion.

Once these five become integrated, you can slowly add others. It becomes a shorthand for e-mail and streamlines everyone's e-mail sorting process.

6. E-mail signature

While e-mail has become the most popular form of communication, it is not always the most effective. When sending an e-mail, be sure to have a signature on the bottom that makes it easy for others to reach you.

In addition to a phone number, consider including your address and links to social media. Depending on your role, making it easier for others to connect with you may improve the odds of getting business done.

Nobody likes to be frustrated by wasting time searching the web to find out how they can contact you directly.

7. Avoid after-hours e-mails

Today's technology makes it easier than ever to stay connected to work 24-7. An idea pops into your head at 9:00 p.m., so you shoot off an e-mail. It gets it off your mind, but what about the recipient?

Have you ever been on the receiving end of after-hours e-mails? How does it make you feel? If it's urgent, it might be understandable. But, most of the time, it is something that could wait until the next business day.

Managers have told me that they instruct employees not to worry about the e-mails they receive outside of a normal workday…that they are not expected to address anything until they are back in the office. If something is urgent, they will let them know.

Why doesn't this work?

Let's assume all employees want to do the best job they can. That includes being responsive. If an e-mail arrives in your inbox at 8:00, 9:00, or 10:00 p.m. and you see it, you are probably going to act on it or at least think about it.

While I find myself crafting e-mails over the weekend, I don't send work e-mails outside of work hours unless absolutely necessary.

Not only is it disrespectful of other people's time, but when you send e-mails outside of business hours, the e-mail is less likely to get the desired response (if it is read at all.)

After-hours e-mail has become such a big issue that as of January 1, 2017, France has enacted a new law, dubbed "the right to disconnect." Firms with over fifty employees are required to set hours (typically evenings and weekends) when employees are not supposed to send or reply to e-mails.

8. Schedule when you send e-mails

Life is about timing.
—CARL LEWIS

What can you do when you have the urge to write an e-mail outside of business hours?

Write the e-mail but delay sending it. Outlook has this feature in its program and Boomerang (http://www.boomeranggmail.com) is a plug-in for Gmail. I use a Mac and purchased a plug-in called SendItLater, now part of MailButler (https://www.mailbutler.io) which enables me to write the e-mail, getting it off my to-do list, and schedule it for a specific date and time.

When you schedule an e-mail, be strategic and send it at a time when it is more likely to be opened and not fall to the bottom of someone's inbox.

I typically schedule e-mails that I've written over the weekend to be sent on Monday morning at 10:00 a.m. Not only does this show that I respect the workday of the recipient, but it is also strategic.

Sending an e-mail at 10:00 a.m. gives someone time to arrive in the office and sort through what is in their e-mail inbox after the weekend. This means that my e-mail is more likely to arrive into a cleared-out inbox and increases the odds that it will be opened and read.

Similarly, avoid sending e-mails at 5:00 p.m. on a Friday when they may get lost during a time when the recipient is more focused on starting the weekend.

9. Pick up the phone

Have you ever experienced the frustration of going back and forth with e-mail just to arrange a time to meet with someone? It may look something like this:

> **You:** Joe, let's meet to discuss the project. Are you free on Wed at 3, Thursday at 10, or Friday at 2?

Joe: Sounds great. Those dates and times don't work for me. How about Wed at 4, Thursday afternoon, or Monday at 9:30?
You: No good. Monday at 2? Tuesday at 10?

I think you get the idea.

What a waste of time! Sometimes we forget that a one-minute phone call might be the easiest way to accomplish what might require a string of four or five e-mails.

Don't be afraid to pick up the phone.

That said, if your work involves a lot of appointment setting, you might want to consider services such as Calendly (www.Calendly.com) or Acuity (www.AcuityScheduling.com) which allow others to self-book appointments with you from time slots you prespecify.

10. Take disagreements off line

Although e-mail is a great and convenient form of communication, there are times when it is definitely *not* the best way to get your message across.

If you strongly disagree with someone, don't write it in an e-mail. For starters, the tone of the e-mail is likely to be misinterpreted. When we feel anger, our writing reflects this and a message of disagreement may come across much stronger than intended.

From a communication and diplomacy standpoint (and to maintain good relationships) we are always best to take a few deep breaths before doing anything. Then, rather than writing a rant, try picking up the phone and having a discussion.

Remember that it is really easy to forward e-mails to a large audience. If you are angry when you write an e-mail, you will not want it distributed far and wide.

11. Get rid of "sent from my..."

While I have heard opposing views, I still believe that it makes sense to change the default message on phones and tablets that says "sent from my..."

If you are sending a work e-mail while you are on the subway or waiting for a doctor's appointment, why let everyone know that you are not working from your office?

I do not believe, as some have argued, that it serves as an excuse for poor grammar or text-like e-mails simply because you are on a mobile device.

If you can't do good work remotely, it is better to wait.

The only valid argument I have heard for keeping the "sent from my..." in the signature, is that it lets people know that when you are responding outside of work hours, it is not your normal workday, and you are simply being ultraresponsive and providing great customer service. It helps to manage the perception that you are at your desk 24-7. Although, essentially, you are.

12. Project-management software

One of the most common complaints I hear is the overwhelming number of e-mails that need to be addressed each day. One way to reduce the volume of e-mails is to use project-management software, like Asana or Trello.

These are particularly helpful when you are working on projects with other people. You can all access information and updates on a project without filling your e-mail inboxes with back and forth messages that may be buried.

These programs offer the flexibility to share folders with different participants, visualize progress, and have both free and premium versions that are robust and easy to use.

If you are interested in giving one of these (or a different app) a try, I suggest you search on YouTube for an instructional video. YouTube videos are a free and great learning tool!

13. Gmail—unsend

For those of you who use Gmail, in 2015 they added a great feature that can save you from embarrassment, shame, and fear—you know, the feelings that surface when you realize you accidentally sent an e-mail to the wrong person (or before you have edited out some inappropriate comments).

To enable this feature, go to the little gear under your profile picture. Click on Settings. Scroll down and select Enable Undo Send. You can select up to thirty seconds to delay the send, and I suggest you take the maximum time.

CHAPTER 2

Communication

*The single biggest problem in communication
is the illusion that it has taken place.*
—George Bernard Shaw

Communication has, and will continue to be, a critical skill for success. Whether you are an entrepreneur or work in a corporate environment, how you portray yourself to clients, customers, and colleagues is highly correlated to your written and verbal communication style.

14. Who is your audience?

Do you fall into the trap of communicating based on your preferred style instead of the person receiving your communication?

Over the years, clients have expressed frustration that employees, supervisors, and clients are simply not responsive.

Sometimes, the issue is that the communication style is simply not the preferred style of the recipient. If you are unsure how your recipient likes to receive information, use trial and error.

If your e-mails go unanswered, try being strategic with the time and day you send e-mails (I like late morning after the inbox is typically cleared out.)

For someone in your office, try a handwritten Post-it note on the computer screen.

Texting is good for getting someone's attention, but not appropriate for sending business communications that someone might need to reference.

Don't be stuck on a single communication style. Paying attention to what gets a quick response will give you insight into the recipient's preferences.

One thing is for certain; hardly anyone checks voice mail anymore. If you don't check your voice mail, you are better off disconnecting it or leaving a message that you do not check voice mail. This way you won't be viewed as being unresponsive.

15. E-mail, don't text

Texting is a great form of communication that implies a sense of urgency. If you are running late to a meeting or simply need to confirm the time you are meeting for lunch, by all means send a text.

As of the writing of this book, texting is limited when it comes to searching and filing communications that might be needed at a future point in time.

So if you think the receiver of your communication might need to look back at it, sending an e-mail will enable them to file it or mark it as unread so they can come back to it. And, if you need the "paper trail," e-mail is the way to go (texts often get deleted en masse to get storage space back on a phone.)

16. Don't wait, communicate

We have all had the experience of working with someone who is difficult or has a temper. It can be tempting to reduce the time you spend interacting with these types of colleagues.

Unfortunately, a lack of communication can often make matters worse. Some people hold in anger, letting it percolate until they explode. You certainly do not want to be the target of this kind of attack.

Projects tend to divert off the straight path we initially plan. When this happens, do not delay to communicate hiccups and new, more realistic timeframes to both colleagues and bosses.

That being said, you are not being paid to have someone else solve your problems. Address the issue at hand, reevaluate, and come up with a proposed solution that is reasonable and gets the job done.

17. Communicate end time

Do you ever find yourself in a meeting that you thought would take thirty minutes but find that the time is suddenly well beyond and is approaching forty-five minutes or an hour?

One of the best ways to protect your time is to manage expectations from the outset. When scheduling a meeting or a phone call, be sure to have both a start and end time.

This reduces the awkward moment when you think the meeting should be over and your colleague launches into a new topic. Meetings are like a gas—they fill the space they are given. To make the most of your time, make your meetings short and communicate the expected duration from the outset.

CHAPTER 3

Meetings

*Meetings are indispensable when you
don't want to do anything.*
—John Kenneth Galbraith

After e-mail, meetings are at the top of the list of productivity-killers. And there is plenty of research to support that this is, in fact, true.

18. Three reasons to meet

There are only three reasons you ever need to hold a meeting:

1. <u>Give or get information:</u>
   I'm not talking about information that could be easily sent via e-mail. This refers to information like corporate restructurings and layoffs that may have staff feeling uncertain and anxious. In situations like this, meetings where senior leaders share information and offer transparency have great value.

2. Discuss options and make decisions:
   Brainstorming with a group can often provide a burst of creativity and ideas that you can't generate independently. Also, when it comes to making some decisions, it is important that the entire group buys into the ideas and results. This also warrants meeting.

3. Building relationships:
   Even in our current digital age, nothing can really replace the human connection you get from an in-person meeting. I have found that when I meet with someone face to face, I am more likely to be hired than from a phone call.

19. Arrive early to meetings

All I do, really, is go to work and try to be
professional, be on time and be prepared.
—BEN AFFLECK

Your initial reaction might be, "Arrive early? Isn't that a waste of valuable time?" The answer is yes…and no.

Let's back up. Suppose you are at your desk and know that you have a meeting down the hall that starts in five minutes. Do you: (a) arrive early, (b) check Facebook, (c) write an e-mail, or (d) make a dentist appointment?

There is a good chance that if you select (b), (c), or (d), you will end up being late to the meeting.

When you show up late, it increases your level of stress, you need to get settled and then you have to catch up on what you have missed.

Overall, by being late you have reduced your ability to be your most effective in the meeting.

If you feel that your attendance in the meeting isn't that critical, so it doesn't matter if you arrive late, it begs the question, "Why are you wasting your time in the meeting in the first place?"

Arriving a few minutes early gives your brain a chance to shift focus to the subject at hand so you can participate fully and add value.

20. Consider alternatives

While a corporate culture might dictate that meetings are the default, it is important to consider alternatives based on your needs.

1. Stand up:
   Could you have a stand-up meeting to cut down on the time? Research by Allen Bluedorn, a professor at the University of Missouri, found that stand-up meetings are about 34 percent shorter than sit-down meetings and yield the same results. The group typically congregates in an area without tables and chairs, which encourages participants to be direct, and to the point. This is a very useful tool for meetings that are expected to last no more than twenty minutes.

2. Walking:
   Another popular option is the walking meeting. This is best when just two people are intending to meet and allows for some movement and exercise, which is much needed in sedentary office environments.

   Steve Jobs, Mark Zuckerberg, and Richard Branson are all known for their walking meetings.

3. Videoconference:
   As technology has advanced, videoconferencing has improved tremendously with clear image and sound to make you feel like you are in the same room. While there are still benefits to meeting in person, if travel becomes an obstacle, a videoconference can be a good solution.

21. Allow transition time

Do you ever fall into the trap of scheduling a meeting that ends at 2:00 p.m. and another that starts at 2:00 p.m.? When this happens, it is inevitable that the second meeting will start late. You cannot be in two places at once. Additionally, your brain needs time to digest the information from the first meeting and reset for the information in the second meeting.

Think of it like high school—there were always a few minutes scheduled for you to get from one class to another. You needed the time to physically move as well as to mentally adjust to a new subject.

This holds true in a work environment as well. Always plan for transition time; even ten minutes will be sufficient.

22. Start meetings at ten after the hour

Have you noticed that most meetings naturally end on the top of the hour or on the half hour? It seems to be human nature that we wrap up at these time increments.

One way you can reduce the amount of time you spend in meetings, is to start your meeting at ten or forty after the hour. When you send out the meeting notification, you might receive some puzzled responses as to the start time, but they'll get the message that you are focused on time and will be more likely to be prompt. Once participants adjust, they will appreciate the shorter meetings.

The other benefit of starting meetings off the hour and half hour is that it naturally builds in a ten-minute window to transition to your next meeting.

CHAPTER 4

Working Smarter

We have all heard the expression "Work smarter, not harder." While it is a little "overdone," I do believe there are ways to make small changes in how you work that can have you producing better quality work in less time.

23. Maximize your windows of peak performance

Have you ever thought about the time of day when you are most alert and productive?

This would be your "window of peak performance." For many people it is early in the morning, a couple of hours after waking. For others, it is late at night when it is quiet, and the rest of the world has gone to sleep.

Whatever your window is, it is important to align your most challenging work with that window. And when you are feeling sluggish (often around 3:00 p.m. or 4:00 p.m. when many go for coffee or a sugary snack), try to use that time for more routine tasks, such as checking e-mail or submitting expense reports.

Being mindful of your window of peak performance improves both your efficiency and productivity.

24. The Pareto principle

In 1906, economist Vilfredo Pareto realized that 80 percent of the land in Italy was owned by 20 percent of the population. Since that time, the 80/20 rule (also known as the Pareto Principle) has been applied in a wide range of areas where it is believed that 80 percent of the results typically come from 20 percent of the input.

Some examples include:

- Twenty percent of your clients provide 80 percent of your sales.
- Twenty percent of your effort completes 80 percent of a project.
- You wear 20 percent of your clothes 80 percent of the time.

In terms of productivity, it is important to recognize that seeking perfection (chasing after 100 percent) can be a poor use of time. If 20 percent of your effort provides 80 percent of the result, chasing 100 percent can be a waste of energy and resources. Spend your time wisely.

If you are not seeking perfection, when do you decide that your work is 'good enough?' You want to be proud of your work product, clear in your communications, and effective in your job.

You should feel that what you have finished reflects positively on you. It's a subjective measure and only you can decide when something is 'good enough.'

As you improve at stopping short of perfection, you will be able to get more quality work done in less time with less stress and a positive outcome.

25. "Done" is better than "perfect"

In software circles, the concept of Minimum Viable Product (MVP) is often used to bring products to market before they have all the features that will ultimately be included. I think of this as another application of the Pareto Principle: Twenty percent of the effort provides 80 percent of the result.

MVP enables developers to release products and websites that have just enough elements to draw in early adopters.

These initial users provide feedback that allows the developers to focus the roll-out of the remaining capabilities at reduced risk and cost.

This approach also helps you avoid "analysis paralysis," a phrase associated with getting so bogged down in details that you lose sight of the bigger picture and don't get anything done.

26. Reduce decision fatigue

A recent Wall Street Journal article, titled *The Cure for Decision Fatigue*, states that by some estimates, adults make as many as thirty-five thousand decisions each day. What to eat, what to wear, which way to turn…the list goes on and on.

It's no surprise that we are looking for coffee or sugar at three thirty in the afternoon. We are exhausted from all the decision-making!

Do you ever wonder why some well-known business titans don't seem to care that they wear the same thing all the time? If I asked you to describe the clothes worn by Steve Jobs or Mark Zuckerberg, I bet you can easily visualize their "typical" uniform.

For Steve Jobs, it usually involved a black turtleneck and jeans. Mark Zuckerberg is often pictured in a T-shirt or hoodie sweatshirt. It might make you think, "Don't these guys care about how they look in public?"

More likely, these are the clothes they are most comfortable wearing. By wearing what appears to be the same thing every day, they reduce the number of decisions they need to make.

I'm not suggesting that you give up your professional wardrobe and wear T-shirts and jeans, but perhaps there are things you waste mental energy on that can be put on autopilot. Like breakfast. Many people eat the same breakfast each day. Why? It's easy and requires little effort.

For the past twenty years, Thursday night has been pizza and salad night in my house. It is one night each week that I do not need to decide what's for dinner. Many people schedule dinners all week long, even further reducing decision fatigue.

Whether it's wearing similar clothes or having the same breakfast each day, we can reduce decision fatigue by putting things that are less important to us on autopilot.

27. Create checklists

Need other ways to reduce decision fatigue? Try checklists. Checklists can be used in many ways—from increasing patient safety in hospitals to packing for vacation. A checklist is a great tool because for recurring events, it takes the mental drain out of the equation.

Here are a few examples of useful checklists:

1. Monthly or quarterly reporting:
   If your job requires you to create reports at regular intervals, a checklist will help you streamline the process. It also enables you to more easily delegate or have someone fill in for you if you are away or unwell.

2. Vacation:
   Do you find that you create a new packing list each time you travel? If you create a spreadsheet with a list of what you are bringing, you can revise it the next time you go on a similar trip. For example, if you travel somewhere warm for five days in the winter, whether you go to Florida or the Caribbean, most of your list will remain the same (x number of shorts, x number of swimsuits, etc.) You can change which shorts or swimsuits you bring, but a checklist will reduce the effort you need to put toward packing. And we all know how hectic life becomes right before a vacation!

3. Supermarket:
   I find that what I purchase in the supermarket is 90 percent the same every time. So I created a master list that goes aisle by aisle based on the market where I do most of my shopping.

I am a little old-fashioned in that I print the list and leave it on the counter in the kitchen so any family member can check off what we need. For items not on my regular list, there are some blanks that can be filled in with one-time items I might need for a recipe or special occasion.

It took about thirty minutes to create the original checklist, but I have been using it for many years with minor adjustments as tastes and preferences have changed.

28. Just say no

Thanks to former First Lady Nancy Reagan's War on Drugs campaign in the 1980s, I'm sure you are familiar with the slogan "Just Say No."

We often forget that it can be applied to other situations that are not good for us or make us uncomfortable. People-pleasers have a particularly hard time saying no.

Time is a precious commodity. You have the same twenty-four hours in a day as everyone else, so it's impossible to do everything that is asked or expected of you. Not to mention that you would like to have some time to yourself.

Every time you say yes to something, you are saying no to something else. Next time when you are tempted to say yes, try saying, "Let me think about it." This gives you a chance to look at everything on your plate (both for work and in your personal life) and make a more informed decision about participating.

29. Delegate

> *Surround yourself with the best people you can find,*
> *delegate authority, and don't interfere as long as the*
> *policy you've decided upon is being carried out.*
> —RONALD REAGAN

In recent years, "delegating" has gotten a bad rap. Often thought of as an opportunity for someone else to dump work on you, people now think of delegating in a negative context.

This is unfortunate, because with so much diversity of talents, skills, and interests, you may forget that the tasks you absolutely abhor might be appealing to someone else. While some of us love working with spreadsheets and details, others among us hate it. Creative work energizes many, but can be scary to others.

If you find yourself with tasks you dread doing, consider delegating this work to someone who enjoys it or is more skilled at that type of work.

Better yet, be proactive in understanding the skills and preferences of your team. When you see an opportunity to provide work a colleague loves doing, you will help to improve their work experience.

30. Time it

Think back to the last time you procrastinated on a task. We often procrastinate on projects that seem daunting, overwhelming, and difficult.

Take a step back and ask yourself, "How long can I work on this task giving it my full attention?" It might only be fifteen or twenty minutes; that's fine.

Set a timer for that interval and get to work. Be sure that all potential interruptions and distractions are minimized (web browsers closed, e-mail and other notifications off). When the timer goes off, take a quick break (use the bathroom, get some water, but stay off social media).

If you feel motivated, do another session of hard work. If not, switch to a less taxing task and come back to the bigger project later.

A Time-Timer (www.timetimer.com) is a simple but useful tool that enables you to visualize the time you have left (there is a red disk that shows the remaining time). I always use a time-timer for my presentations to make sure I finish on time.

There are also many phone and computer applications that provide the same function. A classic kitchen timer or Pomodoro timer also works well.

Francesco Cirillo developed the Pomodoro technique in the late 1980s. This time management system breaks work down into twenty-five-minute intervals with a short, five-minute break. These short sessions of focus with a small break are believed to improve mental agility.

This technique of small, scheduled intervals of focus is also extremely useful for students. I can still remember studying social studies in high school and feeling that I spent thirty minutes looking at the same page in a textbook. Rather than studying, my mind was wandering thinking about how much longer I would need to endure this pain (it was **not** my favorite subject!).

Had I known going in that I was only expected to concentrate for ten or fifteen minutes at a time, I think my studying would have been far more effective!

Nathaniel Kleitman was a physiologist and sleep researcher who discovered something he called the "basic rest-activity cycle," which was based on ninety-minute sleep periods. He found that our bodies operated on ninety-minute cycles during the day as well.

When we try to focus beyond the natural ninety-minute cycle, we find artificial ways to boost our energy (caffeine, sugar, etc.)

According to Tony Schwartz, President of the Energy Project, those who work for three ninety-minute sessions each day are the most productive. These ninety-minute bursts allow ample time for renewal during the day without leading to burnout.

When setting up blocks of time to focus, keep it at ninety minutes or less for maximum productivity!

31. Schedule breaks

Scheduling regular short breaks (ten minutes) can help you be more productive for the following reasons:

1. It helps to get you to places on time. When you arrive late, it increases your stress level, and you may have missed something important in a meeting.

2. It gives your brain a chance to shift gears from one project/ topic to another.

3. It provides an opportunity to change your environment and refocus your attention. Ninety minutes is about the longest time period you can really focus and concentrate without a break and for many people, they are more productive if they take a break after thirty or sixty minutes.

4. It gives you a chance to stretch your muscles if you've been sitting for an extended period of time. It also gives your eyes a break if you sit in front of a computer screen all day.

32. Promise less, deliver more

I like to believe that we are all motivated to perform our best work and exceed expectations. But this can sometimes lead us to be our own worst enemy.

How? When someone asks you to complete a project or task, are you tempted to give them the absolute soonest date you can get it done? We aim to please, but sometimes forget about our other responsibilities and obligations.

When providing or agreeing to a deadline, you need to anticipate potential delays that can arise due to technology glitches or even a medical emergency in your family.

Always allowing a little extra time helps to reduce unnecessary stress. If your assignment is submitted a day early, you will have overdelivered on your promise.

If you cut the deadline too tight and, after a lot of stress and anguish, actually meet the deadline, nobody will recognize or notice your heroic efforts.

33. Avoid music with lyrics when working

One of the more common mistakes you can make is listening to music while doing work.

You may be doing this to drown out the noise associated with an open-floor plan.

Why is it a bad idea? When you listen to music with lyrics, your brain is processing the words you are hearing. If your brain is processing lyrics, it will have a hard time doing another language-based activity at the same time. This includes reading and writing. So, for most people, listening to music with lyrics will impair the quality of their work.

One exception is music that you have heard so many times that it's familiar and your brain automatically puts it into the background.

If you want to wear headphones and listen to music, select one of the many instrumental music options so that the quality of your work will not be negatively affected. A Google search for "productivity music" provides a list of many options.

CHAPTER 5

Distractions and Interruptions

By prevailing over all obstacles and distractions, one may unfailingly arrive at his chosen goal or destination.

—Christopher Columbus

How can you get work done when you are always being interrupted?

You sit down to write the proposal you've been putting off for two weeks. As soon as you get started, the phone rings. An interruption.

Back to work for ten minutes; you're finally in a groove when someone stops by your desk to ask a question. Another interruption.

Back to writing the proposal for fifteen minutes, and you get a text that dinner with clients will be a half hour later.

With all these interruptions, how are you supposed to get any work done?

You are not alone.

Technology notifications and open-floor plans make it nearly impossible to find uninterrupted time to focus on your most difficult work.

"Distractions" and "interruptions" have become very popular answers to the question "What gets in the way of you being your most productive?"

The tips in this section will help improve your productivity in these difficult situations.

34. Do one thing at a time

Faced with a time shortage, we squeeze tasks
into the nooks and crannies of our calendar,
leaving less and less time to switch between them.
As a result, we become less and less productive
exactly when we need to be most productive.
—SENDHIL MULLAINATHAN

Up until recently, multitasking was considered an enviable skill. Science tells us that, at best, 2 percent of the population is actually capable of doing two activities simultaneously.

What we refer to as multitasking, is more often switch tasking where you are rapidly shifting between tasks. You believe that the switching is seamless, but it can actually take as long as twenty minutes to refocus on the original task.

When you switch tasks (think writing an e-mail, answering the phone, and then completing the e-mail), both tasks take longer to complete, have more errors, and you experience greater stress levels.

While you don't always have the luxury of working on a single task at a time, when you have an important project that requires significant concentration, you should unitask, focusing on only one thing. Doing one thing at a time will help to improve your productivity.

I recently came across the paradox (named after fourteenth-century French philosopher Jean Buridan) of Buridan's Ass that illustrates this point. As the story is told, Buridan's ass is equally hungry and thirsty. He is located midway between a bale of hay and a pail of water.

The ass is unable to decide if he should eat or drink first and, as a result of his indecision, he falls over and dies of hunger and thirst.

As humans, we can focus on one thing at a time when needed, even though we are surrounded by distractions. When we allow ourselves to constantly multitask, we are no better than the ass that cannot decide on the one thing to do first.

Try doing one thing at a time, and you will get more things done in less time.

35. Turn off e-mail notifications

I am sure this is not the first place you've read it, but it bears repeating. You need to stop constantly checking your e-mail.

Turning off e-mail notifications (computer, tablet, and phone) is a great place to start. When notifications are on, every visible box that floats on your screen, or ping that indicates a new inbox item, is a distraction.

A study done at the Institute of Psychiatry at the University of London found that this small distraction (even if you do not go check your e-mail when notified) has the effect on your brain as if you have been awake for thirty-six hours or as if your IQ is ten points lower.

Interestingly, this is more detrimental than the effect on your IQ of smoking marijuana!

Simply go into settings on your phone and computer and turn your notifications off. Are you genuinely concerned that you will forget to check your e-mail?

36. Concentrating with an open floor plan

More and more offices are moving to an open-floor plan. Some of the benefits include increased communication, better lighting, and more collaboration among workers.

But there are also issues related to focus that are difficult to overcome. Ideally, companies that have moved to an open plan have also created quiet spaces for phone calls or work that requires significant concentration.

For those who have not, here are two suggestions for getting difficult work done:

1. Find a quiet place outside your office (library? coffee shop?)

2. Wear noise-canceling headphones. Jabra and other brands have created headphones for exactly this purpose. They can be used when speaking on the phone, have an indicator light to let others know you are busy, and have noise-canceling features.

37. Deter interruptions

One of the most common complaints I receive from office workers is that they are constantly interrupted. Sometimes it's someone coming by their desk; other times it's the constant interruption of texts and e-mails.

Interruptions break your train of thought and make you lose your focus.

What can you do?

Interruptions fall into four categories:

1. Important and Urgent
2. Important but Not Urgent
3. Not Important but Urgent
4. Not Important and Not Urgent

Important and Urgent items are typically worth the interruption. Items falling into this category require immediate attention and are probably more important (or as important) as anything you might be working on.

Important but Not Urgent interruptions can be easily handled. Once you recognize that it is something important, acknowledge to the person interrupting that you find what they have to discuss important, but you are currently on deadline.

Would it be possible to meet later today or first thing in the morning? Set a specific time to meet (after all, you did decide that this was important.)

Not Important but Urgent items are the trickiest. This often means that while the task is not important to you, it is very important to someone else. Sometimes, this results from a colleague procrastinating on getting your input for a project that is now close to deadline.

Whenever possible, I believe in helping a colleague or friend to get their work done well and on time. The only exception is if it means sacrificing meeting your own work deadlines. You will need to make the decision in the moment. But helping someone out is a good practice and gets rewarded in subtle but meaningful ways.

Not Important and Not Urgent interruptions tend to be more along the lines of gossip. How was your date? What are your weekend plans? Did you see my Facebook post? None of these relate to work but can consume A LOT of time and interfere with getting work done.

If it's someone whom you'd like to engage in conversation with, suggest that you meet for lunch or after work. Otherwise, explain that you are on deadline and will need to talk with them another time. After a few times, the person should get the hint that you do not have time for idle chitchat.

When you are engaged in critical thinking and want to avoid being interrupted, consider a Do Not Disturb sign or In Conference. Wearing headphones (without music) will give the appearance that you are on a call and cannot be interrupted.

I recently came across an item called DeskMate (available on Amazon) which provides flip signs to let your colleagues know if you are deep in thought or available to engage with them.

No matter how you try and deter the interruptions, rest assured the Important and Urgent items will find a way in if you are truly needed.

38. The twenty-second rule

Shawn Achor, in his book *The Happiness Advantage: The Seven Principles of Positive Psychology That Fuel Success and Performance at Work*, talks about how as little as twenty seconds of effort can deter you from getting started.

For him, having his guitar in the closet (it would take him twenty seconds to get it out) was a deterrent to playing it daily. This works to both encourage and discourage behaviors.

If you are concerned that you watch too much TV, consider storing the remote in a less convenient location. It may not be worth the effort to get it from the room upstairs when your TV is downstairs... perhaps you'll read a book instead.

If you're trying to cut down on sweets, move the candy jar on your desk to someone else's office.

To resist the urge to check your phone during the night, leave it in a room other than your bedroom when you go to sleep.

By making things a little less convenient, you can discourage bad behaviors. And the opposite is also true—making things more convenient can encourage good behaviors.

When Shawn Achor moved his guitar out of the closet, he began playing daily.

CHAPTER 6

Procrastination

> *Procrastination is the bad habit of putting*
> *off until the day after tomorrow what should*
> *have been done the day before yesterday.*
> —NAPOLEON HILL

D o you suffer from the uncontrollable urge to procrastinate? Before you go beating yourself up, recognize that everyone procrastinates at least a little! In my experience, people procrastinate when something seems like a huge undertaking or too difficult to do.

39. Eat the frog

> *Eat a live frog first thing in the morning and nothing*
> *worse will happen to you the rest of the day.*
> —MARK TWAIN

When there are difficult projects or annoying tasks that you don't want to do, try to do them first and get them out of the way.

You usually find that the things you dread are never as bad as you have made them out to be, and it feels SO good to get them off your list.

The sense of accomplishment from doing something you don't want to do energizes you to tackle the more interesting items after.

And if that is not reward enough, consider finding a way to reward yourself for doing the unfun things on your list (set aside time to watch a movie, get a massage, go out for a walk, etc.).

40. Tackle large projects

When something large is looming, it can be really hard to get started. As we delay these challenging projects, they become more and more daunting. It's as if, by ignoring it, it grows into something even greater than it ever was.

What can you do? Try breaking large projects into small, very doable tasks. I suggest creating twenty-minute pieces. With minimal effort, we can allocate twenty minutes of time to even the most boring project.

If the project requires great focus and thought, be sure to assign the completion of a task to a time when you are not exhausted and fatigued. When we are alert and doing our best work, hard work becomes less effort, and we complete things in less time.

41. Don't fear failure

This is a tip I am slowly embracing myself. By nature, I am extremely risk-averse and tend to take the path of greatest certainty.

Of course, the easiest way to avoid failure is to never start...anything. Unfortunately, this is the same method used to avoid success.

In his remarks at the University of Pennsylvania commencement in 2011, Denzel Washington reminded the stadium full of graduates and guests:

> *Reggie Jackson struck out 2600 times in his career, the most in the history of baseball. But you don't hear about the strikeouts. People remember the home runs. Fall Forward. Thomas Edison conducted 1,000 failed experiments. Did you know that? I didn't either—because #1001 was the light bulb. Fall forward. Every failed experiment is one step closer to success. You've got to take risks. If you don't fail...you're not even trying.*

So what does this mean for each of us?

It is human nature to procrastinate on projects and ventures that are overwhelming, difficult, or risky.

Remembering that some of the world's most successful individuals suffered through many failures will help to reduce our fears. Time to get going!

42. Avoid procrastination

We already discussed breaking large projects into small pieces to avoid feeling overwhelmed. Although this is a common strategy, it might not be enough to prompt you to take action.

Another proven approach to procrastinating, is bundling a positive reward with the behavior you are avoiding. For example, if you have difficulty getting to the gym, perhaps you can bring your iPad and watch your favorite Netflix show while on the treadmill or elliptical machine? Or listen to a favorite playlist?

Bundling a positive reward with something you are resistant to do, might be just enough to get you to do it!

43. Balancing current versus future self

To abstain from the enjoyment which is in our power,
or to seek distant rather than immediate results, are
among the most painful exertions of the human will.
—NASSAU WILLIAM SENIOR

One of the most difficult concepts to embrace for both adults and teenagers is the concept that it is worth sacrificing something right now for a benefit that will be realized in the future.

You might be familiar with the Stanford marshmallow experiment conducted by Walter Mischel in the late 1960s and early 1970s. The purpose of the study was to see if there was a connection between the ability in young children to delay gratification for a greater reward and their future success.

In the experiment, each child was given a choice between a small immediate reward (one marshmallow) or a greater reward (two marshmallows) fifteen minutes later if they waited and did not eat the one marshmallow in front of them.

Years later, Mischel and his researchers tracked these same students, and found that the ability to delay gratification when they were little, was directly correlated with academic success (SAT scores) and health (lower Body Mass Index.)

As adults, we know that it is often difficult to put off what we want now for a greater reward in the future. This is especially true when it comes to savings. Foregoing some small luxuries in the present day and investing that money can mean the difference between retiring early and working for longer than you ever imagined.

So, when faced with these trade-offs, don't shortchange your future self. Self-discipline and resisting temptation are difficult.

Find a balance where you can enjoy this very moment but also know that you are taking care of your future self and the needs you are likely to have in ten, twenty, or thirty years.

44. Unpack your suitcase within twenty-four hours

I typically unpack my suitcase within minutes of arriving home. I know it's a little compulsive. And I'm not suggesting you do the same. However, I do think it's helpful to unpack within twenty-four hours, or it may not get done at all.

Like hanging up your clothes as soon as you take them off, unpacking your suitcase means that everything is put back in place and is where it belongs.

There's no need to have yet another thing to do hanging over your head. And, surprisingly, it doesn't take that long!

CHAPTER 7

Planning

It takes as much energy to wish as it does to plan.

—Eleanor Roosevelt

I t is easy to spend our time thinking about what could be and hoping for something to change that will improve our life.

It is nice to dream, and important to have aspirations and goals, but you are unlikely to make your dreams a reality without proactively doing something about it.

A little bit of planning goes a long way.

If you have a goal in mind, think about what needs to happen for you to achieve that goal. What steps can you take to inch closer?

A series of small, little steps feels less intimidating and may help prevent you from procrastinating. Establishing deadlines for each achievement will urge you to move forward.

Celebrating each accomplishment, no matter how small, is an important part of the process.

If your goal is to become a slalom water-skier, you need to acknowledge the process: getting up on two skis, crossing the wakes, dropping a ski, and every other step along the way.

The time and effort that goes into planning and achieving small milestones makes the accomplishment of the greater goal that much more rewarding.

45. Goals

> *You will never reach your destination if you*
> *stop to throw stones at every dog that barks.*
> —Winston Churchill

I bet you have goals that you can identify when asked. But on a daily basis, it is easy to get distracted by the "noise" of everyday occurrences.

We are emotional beings, making it difficult to always have the perspective we need to avoid getting caught up in small inconveniences that can throw us off course.

It could be a comment from your boss that you perceive to be condescending or an indication that he is dissatisfied with your work. Maybe it's the note from your child's teacher that is irritating because you feel it is petty or unwarranted. Or a "look" from a close friend or spouse that makes you feel that you have disappointed them in some way.

These situations can drain you emotionally and distract you from pursuing your goals.

Goals are not just related to achievement in the workplace. Goals can also include the pursuit of healthy, loving relationships with close friends and family.

The above quote from Winston Churchill is a reminder that while you need to deal with the barking dogs, you should try to avoid letting them consume so much of your time and energy that it interferes with you realizing your destiny.

46. Preparation

> *Luck is what happens when*
> *preparation meets opportunity.*
> —ROMAN PHILOSOPHER
> SENECA THE YOUNGER

My father had this quote posted above his desk—it was a philosophy by which he lived.

Thanks to his "organizing" genes, which I inherited, planning comes easily to me. But going from preparation to action can be a big step.

What often gets in the way is a need for perfection. If you are afraid to launch until every duck is in a row, you can become frozen and incapable of moving forward.

If you find yourself in "analysis paralysis," unable to proceed, try to assess if you are at least 80 percent ready (think about the Pareto

Principle I discussed earlier in the book.) If you are, force yourself to move forward. The rest of the details will fall into place.

The other element that attracts increased opportunity is the ability to be flexible. It is the combination of preparation and flexibility that enables you to take advantage of opportunities as they arise and allows 'luck' to find you.

47. Live by your calendar

> *Don't be fooled by the calendar. There are only*
> *as many days in the year as you make use of.*
> —CHARLES RICHARDS

Using a calendar pulls together everything you have going on. Here are four steps to maximize your calendar's performance:

1. <u>One life, one calendar:</u>
   You should have everything on one calendar (both work and personal). If your colleagues can access your calendar, create a separate calendar in Outlook, Google or Calendar (or the system you use) that shows that you are unavailable without providing the detail. This will make it easier for you to get the big picture of your responsibilities and obligations.

2. <u>Use time blocking:</u>
   This is a great tool for protecting your window of peak performance by blocking out time on your calendar to get your most difficult work accomplished. It can also be used for personal routines that you value (family dinners, exercise,

date night, etc.) When items are in your calendar, they are more likely to get done. This is discussed in greater detail later.

3. Assign a time to a task:
   A follow-on to time blocking is to set aside the last ten minutes of each day to assess what you did (or did not) accomplish. Look at the calendar for the following day and be sure to include all set meetings by blocking off the time. Then, schedule in the tasks that must be accomplished, being sure to allow extra time (remember — you can't end a meeting at 11:00 a.m. and start one at the same time.)

4. Follow it:
   Putting everything in your calendar is the first step; then you need to follow it! Use your calendar like a map to get you through the day in the most productive way possible.

48. To-do lists

Billionaires reject the concept of to-do lists.

Successful professionals swear by their to-do lists.

Confused?

You are not alone. There are as many people who declare it absolutely essential to put everything on a to-do list, as there are others who claim it's a complete waste of time.

Don't bother with to-do lists:

Kevin Kruse, author of *15 Secrets Successful People Know About Time Management*, interviewed over two hundred billionaires. His conclusion? Billionaires do not use to-do lists.

As a result, he and others have written articles, books, and blogs cautioning against using a to-do list. They say it is a waste of time.

I challenge this philosophy. Perhaps billionaires don't bother with to-do lists because they are decision makers in huge empires. Their role is to make high-level decisions and put out "fires." I am willing to bet that *all* their assistants have to-do lists!

For many years I did not use a to-do list. Instead, I entered every task directly into my calendar, assigning a date and time to get it done. My calendar was my road map and each night I would print out my daily calendar for the following day.

As small to-dos came up throughout the day, I would jot them down on my calendar printout. I would either complete the task that day or assign a date and time to complete the task when I was in front of my computer calendar that evening.

This system works fine if you do not have too many small, detailed tasks. But looking back, I don't think it was optimal.

You should bother with to-do lists:

We are all getting older. It's a fact. With age, you will have a harder time retaining small pieces of information.

Having a to-do list takes away the burden of trusting your memory. It also frees your brain to focus on important problem solving and critical thinking. We all have so much going on. Do you really want to take the risk of not writing everything down?

While I will not tell you whether you should use paper or an electronic list, there are pros and cons to each. Which you use is a personal preference. But be sure to use something.

Paper: One of the greatest benefits of paper is that when you are writing it helps you to remember. Also, tactile people enjoy the act of crossing items off of their list.

Paper Downside? If you lose your paper to-do list, it can create panic. My suggestion is to take a photo of it with your phone at the end of each day. Then, if you lose the list, the worst-case scenario is that you will have lost one day's worth of entries.

Electronic: The clear advantage is that many apps are free and can also sync across devices. Whether you are at your computer, on a tablet, or using your phone—when a task pops into your head, you can easily record it on your list. The list is automatically backed up, so there is no fear of losing it. Many apps have you check off completed tasks to simulate crossing it off a list. I also like that it is easy to categorize by project, priority, and due date without rewriting your entire list.

Electronic Downside? You lose the benefit of actually writing out the task. For me, it's worth the trade-off to have it electronically. My app of choice is ToDoist; I use the premium version so that it integrates with my calendar and provides additional features.

While a to-do list alone will not get you to accomplish your long list of tasks, integrating a strategically prioritized to-do list with your calendar creates a sure-fire system for being super-productive.

49. Executives

Transitioning into the role of an executive is a challenge. You have gone from managing your own to-do list to a position where you are the go-to decision maker on high-level issues. If you are walking around with a notebook filled with hundreds of tasks, you will feel deflated at the end of the day when you realize that you only checked off two or three items.

As an executive, your role is a combination of visionary (setting the course for future success) and firefighter (making emergency decisions based on your skill, care, and judgment.)

While a to-do list is still important, you need to modify your expectations about performing each task.

Think about identifying the two or three Most Important Tasks (MITs) that you need to accomplish and writing them down before you finish work for the day.

This will keep you constantly focused on what is important and you will sleep better knowing what's in store for the following day!

50. Schedule tasks

Let's say you've bought into the idea that you can no longer rely on your memory and you use a to-do list (paper or electronic).

The scientifically proven, best way to get tasks completed and off your list is to schedule a time in your calendar to get stuff done.

What do I mean? You actually make an appointment with yourself to: go to the supermarket, prepare a speech, write a proposal, or cook dinner. Whatever needs to get done in your life—don't hope that you will have time to do it.

Make the time to complete the things that are your Most Important Tasks by scheduling it in your calendar.

Be sure to leave time in each day for the unexpected interruptions that are likely to come up. Also, leave a few minutes between tasks to either change location or mentally shift gears.

51. Finding flow

> *The best moments in our lives are not the passive, receptive, relaxing times... The best moments usually occur if a person's body or mind is stretched to its limits in a voluntary effort to accomplish something difficult and worthwhile.*
>
> —MIHÁLY CSÍKSZENTMIHÁLYI

The concept of flow was originated by positive psychologist Mihály Csíkszentmihályi and became widespread due to his 1990 book *Flow: The Psychology of Optimal Experience.*

He describes "flow" as "being completely involved in an activity for its own sake. The ego falls away. Time flies. Every action, movement, and thought follows inevitably from the previous one, like playing jazz. Your whole being is involved, and you're using your skills to the utmost."

Some have equated the feeling to a runner's high or a swimmer being one with the water. You may have heard it referred to as "being in the zone" or "the hum" as Shonda Rhimes describes it in her 2016 TED talk, "My Year of Saying Yes to Everything."

It's when you hit that sweet spot and something that is typically challenging becomes almost effortless while, at the same time, you are performing at your best.

It's the state we all wish we could achieve more often! So, how do you get there?

Achieving flow is personal and varies by individual. But we all seem to know the feeling when we have it.

Perhaps it is what you ate for breakfast, how much sleep you had, or the weather outside. Being mindful of what triggers "flow" for you is what will enable you to re-create that optimal environment with greater frequency.

52. Stay fully charged

While this applies to you as well as your electronics, we will address sleep later.

Every night, be sure to charge your phone, laptop, and tablet. Teenagers seem to have a particularly difficult time with this one. I can't tell you how many times my kids' phones seem to have a dead battery right when school ends at 3:00 p.m.

Unless your equipment is old or defective, your battery should have a decent life, especially if you shut down applications that drain the battery. If not, either have it checked out or be sure to carry a charging cord or battery backup with you.

53. Cords to spare

Charging cords can be costly, but purchasing extra cords for strategic locations will save you from the horrible feeling of seeing the dreaded Low Battery warning.

For iPhones, Amazon sells Apple-certified cords that are less costly than the same cord from Apple. There are also very inexpensive (although often unreliable) cords available on eBay.

If you spend a lot of time in your car, invest in an extra charging cord to keep there. Be sure to plug in every time you are in the car for longer drives.

If you tend to be out for the day, carry a charging cord with you; you'd be surprised how many places there are to charge up during the day. But be sure not to leave your charging cord behind!

CHAPTER 8
Time Management

Time management is an oxymoron. Time is beyond our control, and the clock keeps ticking regardless of how we lead our lives. Priority management is the answer to maximizing the time we have.
—JOHN MAXWELL

The term "time management" has changed drastically over the past decade.

Today, Time Management needs to encompass Priority Management, and Attention Management as well. This section will focus primarily on how you can make the most of your time. (Dealing with priorities and attention is covered throughout the rest of this book.)

54. Efficient versus effective

Efficiency is doing things right; effectiveness is doing the right things.
—PETER DRUCKER

While efficiency and effectiveness are similar sounding and often confused, the two have vastly different meanings when it comes to getting your work done.

Efficiency:

Being efficient means you are working in a well-organized and competent way. With so many things to do, it is easy to get bogged down with simply completing tasks on your to-do list.

If nothing else, every time you cross an item off your list, you get a little endorphin rush.

Much like eating sugary, sweet candies, it seems like a good idea when you're doing it. It's only later, when the important and meaningful work has not been accomplished (or you've put on some weight and ended up with a few cavities) that you regret your decision to go for the instant gratification.

Effectiveness:

Being effective means you are successful in producing a desired or intended result. Matching your efforts with the work that requires your unique skill set will result in higher-level performance.

More engaging, more difficult, more time consuming but infinitely more rewarding.

The difference between being efficient and being effective can be the difference between getting a job done or doing the kind of work that gets you promoted.

How can you tell the difference?

Here are some important questions to ask yourself to help distinguish between whether you are being efficient or effective:

1. Am I efficient only at doing unimportant tasks?
2. Am I busy just doing things or am I getting things done?
3. Are the tasks I am working on in line with my priorities?

Focus attention on tasks that help you attain goals. This will ultimately help you find a better balance and become more effective.

55. Perform a time audit

Life and work are full of recurring tasks: doing laundry, performing your morning routine, writing a monthly report, or filling out an expense form.

Performing a time audit helps you better plan and manage your time.

What is a time audit?

When you dive into one of these recurring tasks, track the time it takes to complete. Then, the next time you have the same (or similar) task, estimate the time to complete it, track the time and reconcile any difference.

Over time, you will be able to accurately predict the time it takes for these tasks. Your planning will become more realistic and precise which, in turn, will help you meet deadlines and stay on schedule.

56. Time blocking

When using your calendar to plan your day, time blocking helps you set aside time to get your most important work done.

Some people use time blocking so that they will be assured of uninterrupted time in the office. If your colleagues have access to your calendar and the ability to schedule meetings on it, this enables you to show yourself as busy for the blocks of time you need to get high-focus work done.

Time blocking can also be used more specifically to reserve time for a specific task. For example, if you need to write a proposal that you expect to take an hour, add "Work on Proposal" from 10:00 a.m. to 11:00 a.m.

Do you have personal things that never seem to get done? Try blocking off time in your calendar to do them. This is especially effective with exercise. If your goal is to exercise three times a week, try creating an event (like, Go to Gym) at a specific time in your calendar. There will certainly be times when you need to do something that is more important, but having it as a repeating event significantly increases the odds that you will actually do it.

57. Expect the unexpected—change your mind-set

> To expect the unexpected shows a
> thoroughly modern intellect.
> —OSCAR WILDE

Daily hassles:

Many years ago, I worked with a wonderful client who owns a promotional products business. Let's call her Michelle (not her real name.)

Michelle's primary focus is helping businesses with their marketing efforts by imprinting their name/logo on all sorts of cool stuff (hats, shirts, bags, pens, bottles, etc.)

Michelle expressed frustration that she could not get her work done because she was spending two hours each day dealing with factory errors and/or client demands. Colors were wrong, imprints weren't crisp enough, shipping was delayed, and merchandise was sent to the wrong address. Clients were pulling deadlines forward, changing quantities, and placing last-minute orders.

Every day, troubleshooting issues with both vendors and clients was messing up her schedule.

I spent some time thinking about Michelle's business and some of the daily hassles she had to manage. It occurred to me, that she was great at handling these crises.

Her ability to happily meet the needs of her customers and work through complications with the factories was probably why she has developed long-term, lasting relationships and a loyal following. But something needed to change. Her mind-set!

Changing your mind-set:

My advice to Michelle was to change her mindset. Rather than viewing the troubleshooting as an unexpected annoyance each day, I suggested she embrace it as part of her work.

When planning her day, she needed to set aside two hours that would be spent handling client and factory emergencies.

They would creep in at unexpected times, so she would need to be flexible with scheduling her day. And, if there were fewer issues on any given day, she could simply use the time to begin working on the next day's tasks.

This was an aha moment for Michelle. The source of her daily aggravation was now something she simply expected and handled. If she unexpectedly had a crisis-free day, she would adjust and make use of the newly found time.

Are you in a job where part of each day is spent putting out fires or dealing with daily issues that cannot be predicted? If so, start tracking how many hours each day are spent on these types of tasks.

This will enable you to better plan each evening. If three hours each day are spent on unexpected situations, know that you need to have that time available.

58. Be a satisficer, not a researcher

Some of us are wired to be researchers. Whatever the decision (a car, nursery school, internist, or vacation plans), researchers are compelled to analyze every aspect and angle. Each purchase is viewed as an investment worthy of considerable time and effort to insure that they make the right choice. Consumer reports, online reviews, interviews, and input from peers are sought out prior to any decision being made.

Others of us are wired as satisficers. While also concerned with making the right decision, satisficers spend less time on research and have a greater trust for their instincts. They will do basic, but not extensive, research.

Although studies have shown that researchers usually make better decisions because of their efforts, they are less content than satisficers. This is because they constantly second-guess themselves and wonder if there was information they missed that would have altered their decision and outcome.

I am not sure you can change your natural disposition. If you are a researcher, try to be selective when you follow your urge to explore every detail. Save this skill set for things that matter most.

As a satisficer, I am fortunate that my closest friends are researchers. I am completely comfortable following many of the decisions they have made, knowing that they have been extensively researched and thought through. For me, that is the best of both worlds!

If you are unsure where you fall in the range of satisficers and researchers, there is a great online assessment that provides insight into your natural strengths and tendencies.

The Kolbe A^{TM} Index (forty-nine dollars), found at www.kolbe.com, measures the actions you take and your instinctive way of operating that makes you most productive. One of the four dimensions, Fact Finding, will help you determine if you are more of a satisficer or researcher.

Awareness of your natural inclinations and strengths will help you find flow more often and help increase your productivity.

59. Unknown numbers

Marketers have become savvier making it harder to tell that the incoming call is really spam. You can protect your time by letting unknown numbers go straight to voice mail.

If it's a real call, the person will leave a message, and you can always call them back.

If you realize that the incoming call is spam, you can block the caller on your cell phone to reduce the incoming volume.

To reduce the marketing calls on both your landline and cell phone, consider using Nomorobo.com. When a sales call comes in, the phone rings once and then stops. It has been life changing for our family!

60. Online shopping

If you are a tactile person who likes to touch and feel things before buying, I understand how shopping on the computer may not appeal to you. But shopping online can save you a lot of time and money. So consider it for those things where you can forego touching before you buy.

If you are not already an Amazon Prime member, it is one of the greatest ninety-nine-dollars-per-year investments you can make. Prime members receive free two-day shipping, and sometimes it arrives the next day.

Almost everything you go to the store to buy is available on Amazon and often for a better price. Even if the price is the same or slightly higher, consider the value of the time saved by not going to the store.

When my son moved into his freshman dorm (an apartment with three other boys), I shipped bulk items of toilet paper, paper towels, and Lysol wipes directly to his apartment in Texas. The items were less expensive and having it delivered to his dorm meant that nobody had to lug it from a local Target or Walmart.

When you have a difficult shoe size, ordering online can make the process less painful. Many websites (Nordstrom, Zappos, and often

Amazon) offer free shipping **and** free return shipping. So, rather than be frustrated in a store where you see the boots you love only to find that they are out of stock in your size, you can search online by size first and not be disappointed!

CHAPTER 9

Self-Care and Stress Reduction

*If you ask what is the single most important
key to longevity, I would have to say it is
avoiding worry, stress and tension. And if
you didn't ask me, I'd still have to say it.*
—George Burns

I t sometimes seems easier for you to take care of others than it is to take care of yourself. When you are on an airplane, the flight attendant always makes it clear that you should put on your own mask before helping someone else (even if that other person is your small child or aging parent).

Yet, you tend to put yourself as a lower priority. Doing this can result in greater stress and a lack of well-being. Here are a few strategies to keep in mind.

"Stress" is defined as "a state of mental or emotional strain or tension resulting from adverse or very demanding circumstances."

When we feel stressed, our body perceives a threat to our well-being and releases a chemical that starts the fight-or-flight response. We have all felt it—our heart rate increases, our breath quickens, and our blood pressure goes up.

These days it would be difficult to find an individual who does not experience stress at work and/or at home. While there is evidence that some stress is good for us, prolonged or chronic stress can be detrimental to our health.

61. Perspective

Sometimes we are faced with a stressful situation and our knee-jerk reaction is to panic and overreact. In the moment, it is often very difficult to control our emotions.

However, when we compare the cause of the stress to truly stressful situations (9/11, medical issues, a natural disaster), it can help calm us and keep things in perspective.

62. Exercise

We all know that there are significant health benefits from regular exercise. In addition to being good for your heart and muscle tone, exercise improves the blood flow to your brain, improving your ability to focus. And, while it sounds like the opposite should be true, being active gives you more energy.

Most people are familiar with the endorphin rush that comes from vigorous exercise which makes you feel happy, or even elated. All the positive attributes associated with exercise will result in greater productivity.

Are you having trouble getting motivated? Try making a plan with a friend to exercise together. As of the writing of this book, I am in my fifteenth year of swimming with my friend, Leslie. A lifeguard noticed we swam roughly the same pace and introduced us in 2003. We have been swimming every Monday and Wednesday morning at 8.00 a.m. with rare exception. When the temperature is in single digits and my cozy bed is calling, knowing that Leslie is expecting to see me at the pool is sometimes the only thing that gets me out of bed.

Having an exercise partner also encourages you to work harder and do more. In the fourteen years we have been swimming, we have gotten stronger, faster, and swim longer....and we are fourteen years older!

63. Take vacation

> *I soon learned I could do 12 months'*
> *work in 11 months, but not in 12.*
> —LOUIS BRANDEIS

Why don't employees take all their earned vacation days? Some typical responses might be, "I have no time," "I'm too busy," and "There is nobody to cover my work."

A recent Inc. magazine article, reveals that the average US employee only takes half of his or her vacation time. At the same time, workers are complaining that they are overworked, stressed, and overwhelmed.

Those that go on vacation are very likely to be doing work while they are out of the office. It might be a daily (or more) check of e-mail, a phone conversation, or working on a document.

As our economy has shifted from factory workers to knowledge workers, there is an underlying fear that if we do not make ourselves indispensable, we might be replaced. If everything goes smoothly in the office while we are away for two weeks, maybe the firm does not really value my contribution. Will I be the next casualty in a round of layoffs?

This is faulty thinking.

Here are some of the benefits from taking vacation:

1. Improved productivity:
   Employees who take vacation are less stressed and have lower burnout rates. After taking vacation, workers often find that some of their tasks seem easier than before because they have had some time to relax and let their minds rest. Vacation offers perspective by pulling you out of your daily routine.

   Every now and then go away, have a little relaxation, for when you come back to your work your judgment will be surer. Go some distance away because then the work appears smaller and more of it can be taken in at a glance and a lack of harmony and proportion is more readily seen.
   —LEONARDO DA VINCI

   An Ernst & Young study found that employees who took more vacation performed better on annual reviews.

   Research conducted by Boston Consulting Group found that high-level executives who were required to take vacation were considerably more productive than those who spent more time at work.

2. Reduced stress:
   Taking a vacation and getting out of your everyday routine removes you from the environment where you are feeling stressed and overwhelmed. This gives your body and mind a chance to relax and rejuvenate. Other research has shown that upon returning from a vacation, employees complain of fewer physical ailments.

3. Improved relationships:
   Going on vacation is a wonderful opportunity to connect with family and friends in a meaningful way. In the normal rush of everyday, it is often difficult to have an in-depth conversation with a child, spouse, or close friend. We are all so busy, rushing from one activity or commitment to another. Time off from work enables you to savor new experiences with people who are important in your life.

How do you reconcile being away and things running smoothly without you?

I would argue that the sign of a great employee is one who can create systems and put backups in place that protect the company from his or her absence. Knowledge workers might accomplish many daily tasks, but the real value is in the creative thinking and problem solving that is not easily duplicated.

Taking vacation often falls by the wayside because, although it is important, it is not urgent. Given what we know about the positive impact on productivity and well-being from taking vacation, you need to make sure you find the time to plan an enjoyable experience.

64. Big-picture thinking

One of the most important reasons to take vacation from the everyday is to get some perspective and have the ability to engage in big-picture thinking.

When you step away from your daily routines, you can get a better sense of balance and direction. Are you headed in the right direction? Is this what you want from life?

65. The perfect coffee break

We want to do a lot of stuff; we're not in great shape. We didn't get a good night's sleep. We're a little depressed. Coffee solves all these problems in one delightful little cup.

—JERRY SEINFELD

There are somewhat conflicting reports about the benefits and health risks associated with coffee. Me? I'm a huge fan…even when it's decaf!

How can you have your cup o' joe work best for you? According to a June 2015 article in Time magazine, the optimal time to drink coffee is between 10.00 a.m. and noon or two and five in the afternoon.

The reason is that our natural cortisol levels are highest first thing in the morning. If we drink coffee during this time period, the caffeine interferes with the body's natural production of cortisol, resulting in lower cortisol levels because our body adjusts, relying on the caffeine intake.

See if you can wait just a couple of hours after waking to get the greatest benefit from your morning caffeine boost.

66. Take a nap

For those of you who are unable to manage seven to nine hours at night, taking a nap is a great option for recharging and restoring.

Firms like Uber, Google, Zappos, and PricewaterhouseCoopers have created napping rooms or sleep pods for this purpose.

As the evidence mounts in favor of getting more sleep, other companies are sure to follow suit.

In the current, global economy, you might need to be available at odd work hours for colleagues, customers, and clients in other time zones. Consider napping to get the hours of sleep you need to perform at your best.

67. Ask for help

We sometimes think that asking for help makes us appear vulnerable. While you might be more than happy to offer help, it is sometimes uncomfortable to seek the help of others.

The most successful companies are those whose employees are looking out for the greater good of the firm, not just their own personal success. Being a good team member means not only helping others, but also asking for help when your plate is too full.

The highest achieving employees have the wisdom to know when they need to ask for assistance.

68. Twenty-one days to create a new habit

Successful people are simply those with successful habits.
—BRIAN TRACY

According to a 2006 study at Duke University, more than 40 percent of your daily actions are not based on decisions, but rather on established habits. This means, that by creating new, positive habits, and breaking old, negative habits, you can insure that almost half of your life will be lived well.

January is a popular time for setting goals and resolutions. Studies show that only 8 percent of New Year's resolutions are actually kept. Why is this?

Perhaps, in our enthusiasm for improvement, we create goals that are not realistically attainable. Is it possible that we expect too much of ourselves?

What if you scale back your aspirations to create interim steps toward what you are looking to ultimately achieve? For example, if you are determined to exercise five times a week, aren't you more likely to stick to a plan if you begin with two or three times a week, create that habit, and then add from there?

If you go from never working out to exercising four times a week, haven't you had great success even if you don't reach your goal of five times a week?

Falling short of goals does a funny thing to your brain. It makes you feel like you have failed without giving credit for how far you have come.

The concept of it taking twenty-one days to create a new habit stemmed from the experience of surgeon Maxwell Matz. He noticed that amputee-patients continued to feel phantom limbs until about twenty-one days, at which time their brain seemed to fully process the change.

Since that time, many researchers have challenged the twenty-one-day theory; many believe it takes longer than that to create a new habit. Either way, twenty-one days of doing something can certainly make a big impact and, if you tell yourself it will work and create the new habit, who is to tell you otherwise?

The important thing about creating a new habit is to set yourself up for success. Pick a new habit that will take you less than five minutes a day. We can all find five minutes each day for self-improvement.

Here are a few suggestions (but please do anything that works for you):

Each day:

1. Floss
2. Two thirty-second planks
3. Five push-ups
4. Write down three things for which you are grateful
5. Write down one thing you have done for someone else
6. Get at least seven hours of sleep
7. Meditate for two minutes
8. Don't drink soda
9. Make your bed
10. Don't eat after 9:00 p.m.

Even if you are tempted to do more, start with JUST ONE THING!

It is helpful to print out a blank calendar and cross off each day to mark your progress. As you X out each day, you will notice a chain of continuous days will emerge. As the chain builds, you will not want to break the chain.

This concept of not breaking the chain is often attributed to comedian Jerry Seinfeld. As the story goes, he was asked how he gets himself to write each and every day. He claimed to have a large calendar on the wall where he would put a large red X through each day after he wrote. Soon a chain would develop and he would continue to write each day in an effort not to break the chain.

Sounds hokey? Having completed the twenty-one-day challenge many times, I can tell you that it definitely works. Some of the things I've added to my daily routine: flossing, doing a one-minute plank, pilates 100s, maintaining a gratitude journal, writing one thing I've done for someone else each day, and meditation.

Most of these items just take a minute or two to complete and it's a great feeling of accomplishment and well-being to know that I have created a new healthy habit that I do every day...no matter what.

69. Floss your teeth

An embarrassing truth—I grew up the daughter and granddaughter of dentists, and my brother is a dentist. Yet, I was never taught to floss my teeth as a child and did not heed my dentist's advice as an adult. I have always gone twice a year to the dentist for checkups and, as I have gotten older, the cleanings began hurting more and more. My gums would bleed and be swollen and sore afterward.

Many years ago, I read in multiple publications that it takes twenty-one days to create a new habit. I found the concept intriguing and decided to test the theory.

To increase the likelihood of success, I wanted to select something that is easy to accomplish, would not take up too much time, and did not require specialized tools or skills. Perfect, I thought—let me try flossing.

I have been successfully flossing every day since 2008. I can count on one hand the number of times I have forgotten, and it is usually because I am out of my routine (on vacation). The result? My gums are super healthy, and my semiannual dental cleanings no longer hurt.

How does this relate to productivity? Good dental care will result in fewer missed days of work (not to mention pain and discomfort). As a nice side benefit, your dental expenses are also likely to be less as you find you need fewer crowns and root canals due to your improved oral health.

Isn't that worth two minutes a day? So, if you don't do it already, try flossing each day.

70. Keystone habits

In his book, *The Power of Habit: Why We Do What We Do in Life and Business,* Charles Duhigg talks about keystone habits. These are the habits that, when done regularly, sometimes result in our creating other good habits. The example he uses is that once he became more committed to exercising, he wanted to take better care of his body. The keystone habit of regular exercise resulted in a follow-on habit of improved nutrition.

As you'll read in the next section, making your bed is considered a keystone habit that results in more productive behavior throughout the day.

71. Make your bed

> *If you make your bed every morning, you will have accomplished the first task of the day. It will give you a small sense of pride, and it will encourage you to do another task and another and another. By the end of the day, that one task completed will have turned into many tasks completed. Making your bed will also reinforce the fact that little things in life matter.*
> —NAVAL ADMIRAL WILLIAM MCRAVEN

Mothers have infinite wisdom but sometimes it takes us until adulthood to realize it. Did your mom always nag you to make your bed each morning?

As it turns out, making your bed is linked to the following:

- Increased productivity
- A greater sense of well-being
- The ability to stick to a budget

Thank you, Mom.

So, you might be asking, "How does making your bed increase productivity?"

According to Admiral McRaven's 2014 commencement address at the University of Texas at Austin, making your bed, although mundane and simple, has many benefits.

As the first task of the day, making your bed encourages you to complete more throughout the day. Making your bed reinforces that if you can't do the little things right, you will never be able to do the big things right. And, if you have a bad day and come home to a made bed, (that you made) you will have hope that tomorrow will be a better day.

So if you plan to change the world, start by making your bed.

Need more evidence? According to a study of sixty-eight thousand people by Hunch.com, 27 percent make their own bed, 12 percent pay someone else to make it for them, and 59 percent don't make it at all. 71 percent of bedmakers consider themselves happy, whereas 62 percent of nonbedmakers claim to be unhappy.

Making your bed creates a sense of order, which can positively impact your mental state and well-being.

CHAPTER 10
Mindfulness

Even before smart phones and the Internet,
we had many ways to distract ourselves. Now
that's compounded by a factor of trillions.
—Jon Kabat-Zinn

There has been a lot of media coverage over the past few years about mindfulness and how it is being made mainstream from elementary schools to corporate settings.

Mark Bertolini, CEO of health insurance giant Aetna has become an unexpected champion of the importance of mindfulness. Following a near-death experience, Bertolini radically changed his own health routine and began offering free yoga and meditation classes to Aetna employees.

Employees participating in the program claim a noticeable reduction in stress levels, improvement in sleep, and a decrease in pain. They have also become more effective and productive, translating to an estimated annual benefit to the company of $3,000 per employee.

While mindfulness is most often associated with meditation, that's only one strategy. It encompasses your overall presence and ability to be in the moment. Meditation is credited with being a helpful tool to get you to a state of mind where that is possible.

Through mindfulness, we can focus ourselves to be more 'in the moment' with less worry about the future and fewer thoughts of remorse about the past.

72. Meditate

> *Meditation is a lifelong process. Give it a try. As you get deeper and more disciplined into the process, you'll get deeper and more disciplined in your mind and life.*
> —BRENDON BURCHARD

I was initially resistant to the idea of meditation. I felt that there were too many thoughts racing through my mind, and I would never be able to quiet my brain. In the fall of 2013, I read Kelly McGonigal's, *The Willpower Instinct: How Self-Control Works, Why It Matters, and What You Can Do to Get More of It*, and it changed how I thought about meditation.

The author describes meditation as a strategy for improving focus. In our distracted, digital world, who wouldn't benefit from improved focusing skills? So I decided to give it a try.

When meditating (at least as I will describe it. I am not an expert and recognize there are many methods of meditating), you breathe in and out through your nose. The idea is to inhale deeply and exhale slowly, focusing only on your breath.

This is where you might say, "But, Sharon, there are a million thoughts flying through my head." Exactly.

If you have tried meditating before and thought you were not doing it correctly because your mind wandered, give it another chance. Your mind is expected to wander and it in no way is an indication that you are doing it wrong.

Let the thoughts drift to the side, with no judgment, and bring yourself back to focusing on your breath.

As you do this repeatedly, you are strengthening your ability to get your brain to focus. Imagine how this can help you throughout the day when you are trying to concentrate and other thoughts fly into your head. Pretty great, right?

A few months ago, a friend suggested a mediation app, called Insight Timer. Headspace is also very popular and both apps offer many guided meditation options.

I started using Insight Timer and now use it every day. I find that a guided meditation makes it easier for me to stay focused for longer periods of time and the sound of someone's voice is soothing. There are many options for meditation: if sitting in silence isn't your thing, try an app.

McGonigal suggests that those who are new to meditating start with ten minutes. That seemed like an eternity to me, so I started with two minutes. I committed to meditating each and every day; after twenty-one days, I had created a new habit.

Over time, I have increased from two minutes each morning to ten minutes. It's still below the recommended amount, but this period of time works well for me. Most importantly, start with an amount of time you know you can accomplish and build from there.

My ten-minute meditation provides me with quiet, alone time, each and every morning. It's a small respite from what could otherwise be a hectic start to the day. It enables me to clear my head and start my day with a little less stress and feeling more grounded.

Ultimately, this makes my days more productive.

If my anecdotal evidence hasn't convinced you, perhaps this will:

A group of Harvard neuroscientists studied the benefits of meditation on the brain. Sara Lazar, in her 2012 TED talk "How Meditation Can Reshape Our Brains" shares that past research has shown how yoga and meditation can reduce stress as well as symptoms associated with depression, anxiety, and pain. It also can improve focus and overall levels of happiness.

The results from her lab at Harvard suggest that meditation may actually slow down or prevent the natural aging of certain areas of the brain.

73. Contaminated time

> *Worrying is pulling tomorrow's*
> *clouds over today's sunshine.*
> —CHURCH BILLBOARD IN CLINTON, CT

My aunt Joyce, who is one of the happiest, most optimistic people I know, originally sent me this quote many years ago. She is a wonderful role model for experiencing life by living in the moment.

In Brigid Schulte's book, *Overwhelmed: Work, Love and Play When No One Has The Time*, she introduces the concept of "contaminated time," which is a new twist on worrying.

Do you ever find that when you are in a meeting or waiting in line at the supermarket your mind starts wandering to (and stressing over) what you have to do later that day?

We have all been there. You have so much to do before leaving the office…when will this meeting end?! E-mails, phone calls, quarterly reporting…why is that vice president still talking??

Or, perhaps you are still stewing because the barista in Starbucks got your coffee order wrong this morning. Seriously?! You go to the same Starbucks every day…how hard is it to get a Grande Skinny Decaf Latte with half a Splenda right?

Either way, you are contaminating the time you are in. Your participation in the meeting is marginalized because you are not focused on the content when you are busy worrying about other things. And, the negative energy you are carrying with you from the botched coffee order isn't doing you any good either.

Wherever you are, be totally present and try to only focus on what is being discussed. This conscious state of being is mindfulness.

This can also be applied to the time you spend with your children or loved ones. If you have your phone at the dinner table, you are contaminating the time and not being fully present.

Next time you find that you are not in the moment, ask yourself, "Am I contaminating the time that I am in?" If so, pull your thoughts back to the present and commit yourself to truly being where you are.

74. Follow your moral compass

> *It's easier to hold to your principles 100 percent of the time than it is to hold to them 98 percent of the time.*
> —CLAYTON CHRISTENSEN

On a daily basis, your values and ethics are challenged. If what you stand for and believe in is unclear, being true to yourself can be problematic.

We all have a moral compass. Remember to use it when making decisions and setting priorities. When you put your head on the pillow each night, end your day knowing that you have conducted yourself ethically and in keeping with how you want to live your life.

And if you've gone off course, as we are all prone to do from time to time, tomorrow is a new day filled with endless possibilities.

75. Practice active listening

> *Listening is active. At its most basic level, it's about focus, paying attention.*
> —SIMON SINEK

Have you ever found yourself speaking to someone (at work or at home) and, while you are talking, they are looking at their screen? They are either in front of a computer or their head is down, looking at their phone. You might say, "Are you listening to me?" to which the reply is typically, "Of course I am!"

But they aren't.

Studies show that our brains are unable to do two things simultaneously, especially if those two activities are drawing on the same part of the brain. When you are listening to someone speak and trying to read an e-mail, both of these require you to use the part of the brain that processes language. And it can't listen and read at the same time.

If I am speaking with someone who is looking at a screen, I now wait. I stop talking (it sometimes takes them a minute to realize) and when they look up, I simply say, "I see that you're in the middle of something, we can talk about this later." They usually get the message that I am not willing to compete with e-mail for their attention and they come back to engaging in the discussion.

Remember your mom telling you to look people in the eye when you speak to them? It's good advice and in today's age of digital distraction, it's one of the only ways you know that somebody is actually listening.

So how can you apply this to your life?

For starters, if someone wants to speak with you and you are in the middle of something, ask them to give you one minute so you can finish your thought and clear your head to be completely attentive. And then, look them in the eye and give them your undivided attention.

The other interesting thing about active listening is that it is not the same as engaging in a discussion. When you are actively listening, you are focused on what the other person is saying, *without preparing your next comment.*

When I first read about this, it was a revelation for me. I was always formulating my response when someone else was talking and, as a result, I was missing out on a lot of what they were saying.

Active listeners will listen without interrupting and when the other person stops talking, will ask specific questions related to what the other person has said (as opposed to offering your own experience or opinion).

If you pay attention, you will be able to identify who the active listeners are in your life. They are the ones who make you feel heard and valued.

If you are supervising people, the skill of active listening can make you go from a good to great manager.

Another indication of being present and listening is to put your phone away, with the ringer off, when you are at lunch or dinner with friends or family.

Leaving the phone on the table and having it light up every time a text message comes through is distracting and makes the people you are with feel like you would rather be with anyone but them.

If you want to be heard, take ten minutes to watch Julian Treasure's TED talk from 2013 titled "How to speak so that people want to listen."

76. Coloring

You may have noticed the recent craze in adult coloring books. While I was a little resistant at first (my eyesight isn't what it used to be and coloring within smaller lines is challenging!), I decided to give it a shot.

I bought ultrafine Sharpies in a wide range of colors and a nice coloring book with patterns that were intricate but not so small that I could not stay within the lines with a little effort (and reading glasses).

When I am coloring, I get completely absorbed in the task at hand. I am totally focused on color choice and staying in the lines. It's a form of flow that is meditative and relaxing because there is no room in my brain for other thoughts or worries to creep in.

It takes hours to complete a drawing and when I am done, I like to post them on Facebook.

As an amateur artist, the finished product lacks value to me simply because I did not create the original design. But, unlike drawing the design myself, which I can sometimes find stressful, using someone else's design is completely relaxing and more enjoyable.

If you think back on your kindergarten days with fondness, you may want to give coloring a try as a great way to disconnect and relax.

77. No phones at mealtime

When out at a restaurant, I am often astonished at the number of people who are out socially with friends, and they all have their cell phones out. This sends a message to the people that you are with that, if someone texts or calls them, they will need to disrupt the meal to answer. Basically, the person interrupting is more important than the one you are with at the time.

I have four kids, so I understand that parents are often nervous that there might be an emergency. Aging parents can create the same fears of needing to be reachable at all times. Creating a VIP status for your kids or parents that enables them to ring through when your phone is on Do Not Disturb, can solve this problem.

A kid interrupting a meal with something nonurgent is also rude. More often than not, their texts are not urgent and can wait until after the meal. If you don't respond right away and there's an emergency, wouldn't they call?

When going out to dinner with friends, some young adults have gotten into the habit of putting all cell phones in the center of the table turned face down at the start of the meal. Whoever reaches for their phone first has to pay the entire bill.

CHAPTER 11

Success, Happiness, and Giving

G rowing up in the 1970s, there was an expectation that if you work very hard, you would be financially successful and that would bring happiness. Financial success would provide you with the means to start giving. Evidence has come to light over the past few years to prove that this is not true.

In fact, it is completely backward.

Giving is an attribute that leads to greater happiness and success. Not the other way around.

78. The happiness advantage

90% of your long-term happiness is predicted not by the external world but by the way your brain processes it.
—Shawn Achor

In his wildly popular TED talk, "The Happy Secret To Better Work," Shawn Achor shares the results of his global research from working in forty-five different countries.

The bottom line is that success is a result of happiness, not the other way around.

Achor explains that only 25 percent of job success can be predicted by IQ. The other 75 percent hinges on these three things:

- Optimism levels
- Social support
- Ability to see stress as a challenge instead of a threat

According to Achor, you can train your brain to be more positive and work more optimistically by: expressing gratitude, daily meditation, exercise, acts of kindness, and writing positive experiences in a journal.

79. Small efforts

The quarter in the cart:

Many suburban supermarkets, in an effort to encourage shoppers to return carts to a specified location, require you to put a quarter into a mechanism that releases the cart. When you return the cart, you get your quarter back.

I often find that someone is standing by the string of trolleys when I go to return mine. Rather than retrieve the quarter (or take theirs), I give them the cart and simply ask that they do the same for the next person.

For a mere twenty-five cents, I imagine I have started a domino effect of kindness.

For someone having a bad day, this might be the random act of kindness that shows them that the world can be good.

Certainly, no harm can come from it. As the giver, it makes me feel good to do a small kindness for a stranger. And, from Achor's research, I recognize that this small act probably helps me as much as the recipient.

80. Practice gratitude

> *I don't have to chase extraordinary moments to*
> *find happiness—it's right in front of me if I'm*
> *paying attention and practicing gratitude.*
> —BRENÉ BROWN

Scientific research tells us that repeated thoughts create neural pathways. If you have ever gone shopping for a car, you know this is true.

Let's say you are interested in buying a red Toyota Prius. Once you've thought about it, somehow you start seeing them everywhere—how did you not notice this before? Everywhere you look, there's a red Prius!

The more you identify positive things in your life, the deeper and more pronounced those pathways become.

Starting a gratitude journal sounds like a big commitment. I know because, even though I had read of the many benefits, I put off starting one.

On July 1, 2016, I decided to take the leap. It happened to be my daughter's fourteenth birthday, making my first entry, gratitude for her existence, easy. Every day, I write in a small journal, three things for which I am grateful. I have not missed a day and once you are used to the idea, it becomes easier to find things to write about.

Some days I might write about the beautiful light through the trees or how grateful I am to swim in an outdoor pool in the summer. Nothing earth shattering, just simple appreciation.

With some practice, your brain starts to look for the positive in things...it becomes a reflex. So, even if you feel like you were born or raised a pessimist, you can start to see your cup as being half full and even overflowing.

81. Positive outlook

Being positive can actually improve your productivity. When you think about the people you work with, colleagues with a positive outlook are typically more productive.

We all have bad days. (Without them, how can you measure the good days?) On a bad day, motivation is difficult and everything seems hard.

On the other hand, when you are in a good mood, you are more likely to approach difficult, challenging work with greater confidence. Focusing is easier and you feel stronger and more empowered to tackle the hard stuff.

According to Achor, individuals operating with a "positive" brain are 30 percent more productive than those functioning on brain "neutral" or "negative." Mind-blowing, right?

In December 2016 a study published in the *American Journal of Epidemiology* found that there was a significant link between optimism and reduced mortality risk that was only partially explained by healthy behaviors.

Of the seventy thousand women in the study, the most optimistic had a nearly 30 percent lower chance of dying compared with the least optimistic women.

If you are a pessimist by nature, it might be worth the effort to try and change your outlook through some small daily actions like keeping a gratitude journal, meditation, or acts of kindness to others.

82. "I'll be happy when..."—a recipe for discontent

If you have ever told yourself, "I'll be happy when I _____" (fill in the blank: get promoted, find a life partner, lose weight, etc.) then you have probably found yourself disappointed.

When we select events that will make us happy, once we reach them, we simply move the target. And then we decide we will be happy when we get the next promotion, lose another ten pounds, or get an even bigger house. It becomes a never-ending cycle of unhappiness, discontent, and disappointment.

Rather than linking happiness to success, we need to create daily routines that raise our level of happiness.

83. Give

> *My father said there were two kinds of people*
> *in the world: givers and takers. The takers*
> *may eat better, but the givers sleep better.*
> —Marlo Thomas

Each holiday season, we find ourselves in a giving and generous mood. We say we are in the holiday spirit. Imagine a world where that spirit of generosity continues all year long.

Adam Grant, in his book *Give and Take: Why Helping Others Drives Our Success,* discusses many of the benefits of being a giver.

According to Grant (the youngest tenured Wharton professor), we generally fall into one of three categories: giver, taker, or matcher.

Takers feel no shame in taking what they can get with no obligation to give or help others in return.

Matchers live to be fair—you help me and I'll help you…to the same extent.

Givers tend to give because they can, with no ulterior motive.

To give without the expectation of anything in return feels good and puts a positive energy into the world.

One of the most interesting examples of this is Adam Rifkin. In 2011, Rifkin was named as Fortune's Most Connected Man based on his LinkedIn connections to the 640 most powerful people on Fortune's lists.

How did he do it?

Rifkin, an entrepreneur, had a habit of giving. Through small acts of kindness and generosity, he developed a network of people who connected him to others. These connections resulted in investments in his businesses by venture capitalists.

He, in turn, continued to advise others and connect people in his ever-expanding network. Most people would agree that it simply feels good to help someone. Reading Grant's book heightened my awareness and made me want to strive to be more of a giver.

Wouldn't it be great if we can all refocus our efforts to give a little more with no expectations in return?

What can you take from all of this?

Don't look to financial success to make you happy; you won't find it.

Happiness results from some simple but basic daily routines. Putting a little effort into looking for the positive, helping others, being mindful of what is good in your life, and taking steps toward showing appreciation and kindness will increase your level of happiness.

And then, there are no limits to your success!

CHAPTER 12
Evening Rituals

84. Ten minutes of planning

One of the best gifts you can give yourself is to spend ten minutes toward the end of the day planning for tomorrow. Use this time to review any items that did not get done that you had intended to complete during the day. These tasks need to go back on your to-do list and be reprioritized.

Once you have an updated task list, look at the following day's calendar. Be sure all set meetings and appointments are booked. Then, leaving a few minutes between each task/meeting, schedule in time to complete your most important tasks.

If you have a job that requires you to handle crises that come up each day, make an estimate of how much time you spend on these unexpected surprises each day and block out that much time. For example, if ninety minutes each day is spent 'putting out fires,' be sure that you only schedule eight and a half hours of a ten-hour day. And don't forget lunch!

Having a plan in place each evening will help you sleep better at night because you will go to bed with a clear idea of your next day's priorities.

Especially in today's global economy, you might wake up in the morning to find that something occurred overnight, and your priorities have shifted. Because you had planned ahead of time, your priorities are clear, and you will have the ability to be flexible and resilient to handle new challenges and stresses as they present themselves.

85. Lay your clothes out the night before

In an effort to reduce decision fatigue, try laying your clothes out the night before.

A simple check of the weather will ensure that you are dressed appropriately. If you're concerned, you can always check again the morning before getting dressed to see if the weather has changed drastically.

Why lay your clothes out? Mornings are usually rushed. I still remember getting dressed in the morning before middle school and going through many outfits before finding the one I felt comfortable wearing. It was almost forty years ago, and I can vividly recall how stressed it made me feel. Once I began laying my clothes out each night, the overwhelmed feeling of what to wear simply went away.

Friends and family sometimes make fun of me for it, but I also do this on vacation.

Having one less decision to make first thing in the morning will help you stay on track and arrive on time. Although you might be fatigued at night, selecting clothes doesn't typically require too much intense thought.

86. Go to sleep

I know, I know—you probably think I've lost my mind. You need to get work done! How can you possibly go to sleep at a reasonable hour?! Besides, since college, you have been well trained to get by on less sleep. By now, you've mastered the art of sleeping less and doing more.

I've got bad news for you. You are kidding yourself if you think you can get by on little or no sleep.

In her book, *Thrive: The Third Metric to Redefining Success and Creating a Life of Well-Being, Wisdom, and Wonder*, Arianna Huffington describes her 2007 wake-up call. She was so exhausted and sleep deprived that she collapsed, hitting her head on the desk, resulting in a broken cheekbone, a cut eye, and a lot of blood. This caused her to take a good, hard look at her life and reassess her priorities. It also prompted her to write this book!

She discusses a variety of lifestyle topics including stress, meditation, and sleep. Huffington quotes Drs. Stuart Quan and Russell Sanna from Harvard Medical School's Division of Sleep Medicine who found that "sleep deprivation negatively impacts our mood, our ability to focus, and our ability to access higher-level cognitive functions."

Interestingly, she also mentions that according to a study in *Science*, those who are sleep deprived have a greater boost in their level of happiness from an extra hour of sleep than from a $60,000 raise!

A 2013 Gallup poll found that 40 percent of Americans are not getting enough sleep. (Experts recommend seven to nine hours a night.)

In 1942, 8 percent of those polled (versus 26 percent in 2013) got six hours of sleep and 45 percent (versus 29 percent in 2013) got eight hours. Three percent reported less than five hours a night in 1942; that number was 14 percent in 2013.

What happens when you are sleep deprived?

In addition to finding it difficult to focus, your cognitive abilities become impaired. This means you will be slower in getting work done, less creative in your problem solving, and more prone to making mistakes. You end up spending more hours doing poorer quality work.

It's hard to imagine, but if you got a better night's sleep, you would need to spend less time getting the same work done...and the work you do would be better!

87. Keep pen and paper next to your bed

Even if you are diligent about planning the following day each evening, you might find your mind racing at night as soon as your head hits the pillow.

This can cause anxiety, sleep issues, and worries over what you must remember for the following day.

A quick and easy solution is to keep a pen or pencil and paper on the nightstand next to your bed. I like to keep an index card because it is small and unlikely to fly off during the night when adjusting my blankets creates a small breeze.

In the morning, I always check my nightstand in case I have written a note to myself.

Having these tools handy to capture your thoughts means you can unburden your memory and let your brain rest through the night, providing a better night's sleep.

88. Don't sleep with your phone

Let me guess….you sleep with your phone because it's your alarm clock. Do yourself a favor, spend a few dollars and buy yourself an alarm clock that is not your phone. I recently purchased a new one (the prior one had a CD player that I never used and it was taking up space on my nightstand). For about twenty dollars, I purchased a radio alarm clock that enables me to wake up to birds chirping or the sound of rain!

Why is it a bad idea to sleep with your phone?

For starters, the blue light emitted by laptops, cell phones, and tablets will disrupt your sleep. To me, even more important than that, is that if you sleep with your phone by your bed, you will be tempted to check it constantly.

Be honest. When you get up in the middle of the night to go to the bathroom, don't you think, "Oh, I'm up anyway; let me just check my e-mail or see if anything exciting has happened on Facebook"?

We are already struggling with our cell-phone addiction. A good place to begin breaking the habit of constantly checking is by leaving your phone to charge in another room when it's time for bed. You will sleep better, and it will be a daily reminder that you can separate from your phone and nothing terrible will happen.

Worried that you'll miss an emergency phone call? Here are two possible solutions:

1. Put your phone on "Do Not Disturb" in the next room, but allow your VIP callers to ring through.
2. If you still have a landline, be sure that your closest family and friends have it in their phone. Let them know that if they can't reach you on your cell, they should call your landline.

89. Reduce blue light

You know that your computer's blue light is bad for your sleep. Ideally, you want to avoid these screens before bedtime. Realistically, that won't work for everyone.

One great solution is the website justgetflux.com.

This free service enables you to download an application that will adjust the blue light of your computer screen at dusk and at night. The screen turns a slightly orange color, which takes some getting used to, but it will significantly reduce the amount of blue light and enable you to sleep better.

According to their website, "During the day, computer screens look good—they're designed to look like the sun. But, at 9 p.m., 10 p.m., or 3 a.m., you probably shouldn't be looking at the sun. f.lux fixes this: it makes the color of your computer's display adapt to the time of day, warm at night and like sunlight during the day."

If you know you can't resist the urge to use your computer before bedtime, at least give this a shot.

CHAPTER 13

Self-Development

Don't ask what the world needs. Ask what makes
you come alive, and go do it. Because what the
world needs is people who have come alive.
—THEOLOGIAN HOWARD THURMAN

We are all born with talent, but sometimes it takes a while to discover our purpose and passion. As it turns out, pursuing our interests leads us to practice and master what we love.

This building of skills is part of what makes us unique and special. Our innate, God-given talent is a gift, but it is up to each of us to find, nurture and develop it, to maximize its potential.

90. Increase your grittiness

Grit is that 'extra something' that separates
the most successful people from the rest. It's
the passion, perseverance, and stamina that

we must channel in order to stick with our
dreams until they become a reality.

—TRAVIS BRADBERRY

In her book (and TED talk), *Grit: The Power of Passion and Perseverance,* Angela Duckworth defines "grit" as "perseverance and passion for long-term goals."

Her research suggests that grit (as opposed to IQ, social intelligence, or talent) is a positive indicator of future success. Those who have the ability to stick-with-it and stay motivated over long periods of time are thought to be gritty.

These individuals are undeterred by failures and setbacks. How can you be grittier? If you believe you have the ability to learn and grow, you develop a growth mind-set, which is more likely to result in grit.

So, when things don't work out the first time, don't be too discouraged. Pick yourself up and try again…and again.

91. Lifelong learning

My teenagers can't wait until they are done with school. They are tired of having to study and take exams. They are sick of being constantly judged through the grading process.

But what about learning, not for grades, but to build your skill set? With the widespread availability of online courses (both free and for a fee), it is important and easier than ever to continually learn and develop.

Stanford University professor, Carol Dweck, researches the concept of "growth mind-set," the belief that you can grow and develop your brain's capacity to think and solve problems. Having a growth mind-set is often thought of as a predictor of success.

If we do not continue to grow and challenge ourselves, our knowledge base becomes stale and dated.

I have enjoyed taking a number of Massive Open Online Courses (MOOCs.) Although I knew of the concept (free online courses offered from top universities around the world), I only recently began to take advantage of this unique way to learn.

What I like most about this format is that most lectures are less than ten minutes; it is the rare lecture that exceeds fifteen minutes. And, because I am easily distracted on the computer, I found that by increasing the video speed to 1.25× or 1.5×, I am forced to give the lecture my full attention. This prevents me from giving in to the impulse to check e-mails or work on my to-do list while I'm learning.

Most courses run four to six weeks and I commit about two to three hours a week to cover the material. The courses have weekly quizzes to confirm that you have mastered the content (but don't worry, they give you many opportunities to retake the quiz if you don't pass initially).

For those motivated by credentials, there is an option to purchase a certificate for a small fee at the completion of each course.

Coursera, the largest platform, was started in 2012 by two Stanford professors. The course offerings are from some of the world's top professors and universities. Most platforms offer apps so you can learn on a phone or tablet as well.

If you can find the time, learning through a MOOC empowers you with knowledge and is a great use of time.

From social media marketing at Northwestern, to negotiating at Yale and Positive Psychology at UNC, Coursera has allowed me to broaden my horizons with nothing but a computer and Internet connection.

Why not challenge yourself to learn something new? It is empowering and confidence boosting!

92. Pursue hobbies

I'm sure you're familiar with the proverb "All work and no play makes Jack a dull boy."

I believe that we should all find work that we enjoy doing. I am not a fan of taking a high-paying job in a very stressful environment, with the intent of working really hard for x years to make a lot of money so you can then pursue your passion.

But you also need to recognize that not all hobbies can become careers. There needs to be some middle ground.

We spend too much time at work to stay in a place that is making you miserable (whether it's your boss or that you despise the actual work you are doing).

On the other hand, it's called work for a reason.

And, if you are in a job that you love, it's still important to develop some interests unrelated to your career. Otherwise, you become singularly focused and, quite frankly, dull.

Hobbies help you develop a new skill area, and it gives you something interesting to talk about (especially when you are networking or on a job interview.) Extracurricular activities can often be the common bond that helps you to connect with a new friend or colleague enabling you to widen your networking circle.

This is probably why golf has become such a popular activity among business people.

Finally, pursuing a hobby can help to improve your problem-solving capabilities. How? When you do something different, engaging another part of your brain, you allow your brain to think differently. It can give you a new perspective.

93. Accept criticism

I like criticism. It makes you strong.
—LEBRON JAMES

When I read Peter Bregman's book, *4 Seconds: All the Time You Need to Stop Counter-Productive Habits and Get the Results You Want*, I found the section on accepting criticism particularly helpful.

My personal tendency is to blow criticism out of proportion. It takes a while for me to stop being defensive and analyze what I'm being told so I can change and improve.

While you can't please everyone all the time, and some criticism might be exaggerated, I believe there is some truth in every comment. This is sometimes masked by the way in which feedback is delivered, which can often be harsh and hurtful.

Most people are nonconfrontational. This means there are times when your behavior irritates or annoys others but they say nothing. Instead, they simply avoid you or choose not to do business with you. Looked at this way, criticism can be viewed as a gift.

Here are four ways we can be more open to criticism:

1. Set aside emotions:
   Receiving criticism can hurt your feelings. Setting your emotions aside means you can be more open to truly listening to what is being said.

2. Focus on what is being said, not how:
   If you have ever provided feedback, you know that it is not easy to relay a message without sounding critical. Always remind yourself to focus on the message, not the delivery.

3. Listen:
   Your first instinct might be to justify your actions. But regardless of intent, perception is reality and the person providing feedback may have interpreted something you did in a way you did not intend. You need to listen and ask questions to fully understand their concerns.

4. Plan action:
   When you have absorbed the criticism and are no longer emotional about it, you can think about ways to improve in the future. Are there specific steps you can take to reduce the chance this will happen again?

I don't know anybody who likes to be criticized. But I also believe that most professionals are looking for ways to receive feedback so they can continually improve themselves and their performance.

The gift of feedback enables you to know where you should focus your efforts.

94. Network

> *I think women are really good at making friends and not good at networking. Men are good at networking and not necessarily making friends. That's a gross generalization, but I think it holds in many ways.*
> —MADELEINE ALBRIGHT

One of the greatest benefits of the digital age is the increased ability to maintain your network.

But networking is more than liking someone's post or commenting on an article; it's continuing or developing a real relationship.

Social relationships enable you to build trust and trust builds business. Whether you have a product or service to sell or are looking for employment, connections are the most reliable path to success.

Attending networking groups or setting aside time to meet a colleague for coffee requires time. Be sure to plan weekly and monthly networking opportunities. If you wait until you need your network, it might be too late.

When someone contacts you to network, find some time, even if you are busy. A fifteen-minute phone call or quick cup of coffee might enable you to provide much needed advice or connections that have a great impact on someone else's career.

CHAPTER 14

Community

95. Give credit

> *No man will make a great leader who wants to do*
> *it all himself, or to get all the credit for doing it.*
> —ANDREW CARNEGIE

It sounds simple and you might think you already do it, but giving credit is so important. We've all been there...you work really hard on a project. Your boss loves it. The client loves it. And, while it may have been a team effort, your boss's boss seems to take all the credit. It doesn't seem right, and it doesn't seem fair.

You can be different. Whether you work for someone else or have your own company, giving credit and thanking people for their work will always serve you well.

We all like some recognition, especially when we work hard. Expressing gratitude and giving credit cost you NOTHING. Interestingly, it will also help you be more productive since people are happier and will work harder for you when they feel appreciated.

96. Be part of the community

Life is not accumulation, it is about contribution.
—STEPHEN COVEY

There are many ways to define one's community. No matter your definition, being an active participant in a community is good for your heart, soul, and productivity.

Volunteering should be done for the right reasons. Find a cause about which you are passionate. Whether it's a school, community center, religious congregation, or local food pantry—it needs to be something you genuinely care about.

The amazing thing about being part of a community is that you are able to connect with a group of people who are passionate about a common cause. This creates a sense of meaning and purpose that is hard to replicate.

This also builds a network of like-minded people who are giving by nature. What a great opportunity to exchange ideas, offer support, or suggest resources that can be helpful to everyone.

97. Use your alumni network

As human beings, we look for ways to connect with each other. One easy and comfortable way to do this is through the alumni network of your college or graduate school.

Whether you are seeking some help or have the ability to help others, alumni groups are a great way to connect in a nonthreatening environment.

You already have something in common with the people who you will meet, which makes it easy to start conversation (even for us introverts).

Your college degree also provides a point of reference, which is why people often hire from their alma mater.

Contact your school and find out about programs in your area. You might also want to consider volunteering as an alumni interviewer or be a member of an event planning committee.

CHAPTER 15

Simplify

98. Unsubscribe from catalogs

E very time you order from a catalog or online, your name and address gets put on that store's mailing list as well as the other retailers with the same parent company. Your name and address are also likely to be sold and end up on other mailing lists for retailers looking for a similar customer profile.

While online shopping has exploded in the past five to ten years, it seems that the number of catalogs we receive in the mail has not diminished.

To unsubscribe from unwanted catalogs, try using CatalogChoice. com. This free service will enable you to easily get off of many mailing lists.

If you are trying to stay within a budget, then unsubscribe from everything. If you need something, you surely know where to go. Receiving catalogs with promotions and sales plastered all over the cover gets you to look and buy things because they are a "great deal," not because you actually need these things.

Save yourself some money and your mail carrier's back—unsubscribe from as many catalogs as possible.

99. Unsubscribe from magazines and newspapers

Have you been receiving the same magazines for years or decades? Do you find that they pile up until you finally binge read them or give in and recycle them?

You may have subscribed to magazines at a time in your life when you had more leisure time to read. And you loved your magazines: *Glamour, Time, People, Cosmopolitan, The New Yorker, Popular Mechanics,* etc.

With your attention being divided in so many directions, you need to be more deliberate about the magazines and newspapers to which you subscribe.

In addition to the clutter they create, there is no reason you should feel guilty about not having the time to read everything that gets sent to you.

Personally, I have gone in and out of reading the *New York Times* on a daily basis. I enjoy doing the Ken Ken and crossword puzzle but was only reading the paper a few days a week.

When the paper would go untouched into recycling, I'd feel a twinge of guilt. So, I subscribed to get the puzzle as well as the *NY Times* daily e-mail digest in my inbox each morning.

Now it is easy to read the news each day (the one-pager is enough for me), and I get to do the crossword. I saved money and reduced a lot of paper clutter in my home.

Is there a better solution for your newspaper and magazine subscriptions?

Instead of automatically renewing, be deliberate in your actions.

100. The news

There is so much information at our fingertips that if you love information, you could get lost for the day just reading the news.

On the other hand, due to the accessibility of news, there is an expectation that you know what's going on by the time you start your workday.

How can you simplify?

If you are a person who needs to read a paper cover to cover, this won't be enough for you.

But for those of you who want the facts and enough information so you can speak intelligently with colleagues, here are two great resources:

1. The *New York Times*:
   The *New York Times* offers free e-mail newsletter subscriptions. You can choose from a wide range of topics and locations. I receive the Morning Briefing for the Americas and find that it fills me in on what I need to know. You can subscribe at www.nytimes.com/newsletters/morning-briefing.

2. The *Skimm*
   I also subscribe to the *Skimm*, another free daily e-mail. While the stories tend to overlap, the *Skimm* is written in a very clever way and includes some pop culture, which I enjoy.

Both of these e-mails arrive in your inbox by about 6:00 a.m. each weekday.

I am sure there are many other options available as well. The important thing is to find something that is simple, not too time consuming, and provides you with sufficient information.

101. Pay online

One of my pet peeves is writing out checks. I know it's not a big deal, but I have always found it boring and cumbersome. Filling out a check register to make sure my statement balanced each month was yet another hassle that I did not enjoy.

And then online banking hit the scene. Once you get comfortable with any security concerns you may have, online banking is fantastic. Paying bills is much quicker (no envelopes, stamps, or writing out checks).

And, even more current than online banking, is Venmo. This fantastic app lets you pay people in the absolutely easiest way possible. If you are not already a Venmo user, I suggest you look it up. I think most millennials use it—it is simply the most convenient way to get money to someone.

102. Paperless, electronic statements

Isn't it surprising how much mail still comes each day, even though we are in the digital age?

Getting bank and credit card statements online will greatly reduce the amount of paper you need to handle and manage.

Many clients have expressed concern about not receiving physical statements. What if something happens to the bank? Suppose the Cloud crashes?

The concerns are certainly valid. One work-around is to download the pdf statement each month when you receive the e-mail notifying you that your statement is ready.

PDF files do not take up a lot of space, and you can easily create a filing system by year for each account. It takes less than two minutes to download and file the pdf, and it will give you peace of mind that you actually have all of your statements and do not need to rely on your bank's server and Cloud storage.

103. Books

Do you have a hard time saying goodbye to your books? If so, you are not alone. I have rarely worked with a client who did not feel a deep emotional attachment to the many books collecting dust on the shelf.

Many of us were raised to believe that books are sacred—they should be handled carefully and not be written in! Unfortunately, when you collect hundreds of books, your home or bookcases become cluttered, the books are rarely reread, and the dust begins to build. For those with asthmatic tendencies, this can be particularly bad.

What can you do?

For starters, it's important to remember that you can always take a book out of the library (or download it). While there are occasionally first-edition books that have some value for collectors, most books are not collectibles and the value is mainly sentimental.

It is easiest to start with novels. If you have a few novels that you might actually read again (Atlas Shrugged falls into that category for me), set them aside. The rest of the novels can be donated. Many local libraries collect books throughout the year or shortly before they have a sale. Call around; it always feels better to donate than put a book in recycling.

That being said, nobody really wants very old books (you know, the ones that are red or yellow on the side with a cover that is crumbling). If you have some of these types of books feel free to pick a favorite or two to put into a memory box (see strategy #117 for information on memory boxes). The rest should be recycled...I know it's painful.

Many libraries will not accept textbooks and encyclopedias so check before you lug them over.

There are many options for book donation that can be found online, so be sure to take a look if your local library is not the best alternative for you.

There are programs to send books to:

1. Soldiers (http://booksforsoldiers.com/donate_to_the_soldiers/)
2. Students in Africa (http://www.booksforafrica.org/books-computers/donate-books.html)
3. Prisoners (http://www.bookstoprisoners.net)

These are just a few examples of creative ways to find a new home for your treasured book collection.

After sorting through novels, look through resource books, textbooks, etc. Only keep what you think you will actually use or the books that you absolutely love to see on the shelf.

This will free up your bookshelves for decorative items as well as some free space. You will see how much less dusting you will need to do!

104. Duplicate toiletries

Do you shower at the gym? Travel often?

If so, one simple thing you can do that will save you a lot of time and effort, is create a duplicate toiletry bag (and make-up bag if you choose).

While it is a bit of a hassle to buy everything you need (and in travel size if you intend to take it on the plane), it makes life much easier. When you pack, you simply grab the bag.

When you return from a trip, be sure to check your bag for any items that need replenishing. Making this part of your coming-home routine will avoid the annoyance of not having something when you need it and are away from home.

105. Delivery

If you are still spending a lot of time running to the dry cleaner and supermarket, it's time to stop. Most urban and suburban communities offer free pick-up and delivery of dry cleaning. What a tremendous convenience! If your timing is tight, some services will try to accommodate a rush order as well.

For groceries, there are more and more local supermarkets as well as grocery delivery services (without a storefront) that provide exceptional service. While you may need to pay a delivery fee, think of what you are saving in time and physical labor.

In the suburbs, when you go to the supermarket, you select each item, put it in your cart, then put everything on the belt at checkout, then pack each item into bags, then put the bags into your cart, and then load the bags into your car. You drive home, take out all the bags and have to then unpack them. Just thinking about it makes my back ache!

Imagine the convenience of selecting items on your computer, they arrive at your door, and you simply unpack the groceries.

For those of us who like control, this can be a bit scary. Someone else is checking to see if the cantaloupe is sweet and the avocado ripe. If you are able to let go a little bit, you will be greatly rewarded by recouping A LOT of free time.

I also believe that I have far fewer impulse buys if I am not in the store. When I am tired and try to tackle a big shop at the supermarket, it takes longer, and I succumb to impulse buys. (I am weakened with exhaustion and have no fight left to stay focused on the list of what I really need.)

To me, what I save by shopping from home more than covers the delivery fee. Try it!

CHAPTER 16
Backups

106. Scan photos

I n 2010, my town felt the impact of hurricane Irene, leaving us without power for four days. It was a time when I became extremely close (literally) to my husband, four kids and dog, by sleeping huddled in front of our gas fireplace.

It was also a time to reflect on what possessions I cherished most.

On the first day of the storm, the heavy winds caused a downed wire in front of my house that caught fire. As I watched it creep closer to my home, I could not help but think, "This is a defining moment. If I have only five minutes to evacuate my home, what will I take?"

After grabbing my grandmother's candlesticks, my next thought was to rescue my photo collection.

I had already accomplished the dreaded task of pulling apart old albums, sorting by date, and filing them in photo boxes. But I still had over four thousand photos in boxes. So I had my kids help me load them in the car.

When the storm passed and life returned to normal, I spent some time thinking about that defining moment.

I was fortunate that I did not need to evacuate my home and my belongings were unharmed. With the more frequent occurrence of severe storms, I decided I did not want to risk losing my photos again.

So I began the tedious process of sorting through all my pictures, getting rid of duplicate and blurry images. I scaled my collection down to three thousand and sent them all to be scanned.

After a great deal of effort, sorting and key wording, I now have the most useful photo library with over thirty-five thousand images (with digital photography, it's grown quite a bit since 2010). Photos of every member of my extended family can be searched for by name.

My photos are all kept on a physical external drive, which is backed up both onto the Apple Time Machine in my home and to the Cloud by CrashPlan.

I no longer worry about losing my photos and my kids love that they can access all of our family photos, including those from my parents and grandparents going back to the 1940s.

107. Back it up

You have probably been told that it's a good practice to back up your computer and phone on a regular basis. Do you?

Years ago, you needed to take action to back up either by plugging into an external drive or waiting for your firm's weekly automatic backup.

The good news is that we've come a long way. Cloud storage has become extremely affordable and is often automatic. Once you have a system in place, you do not even need to think about it unless your hard drive crashes and you need to restore your data.

Services like CrashPlan and Carbonite are Cloud-based options that cost as little as sixty dollars per year. Unlike an external drive on your desk, if your office burns to the ground (which, of course, is a worst case scenario), your data will still be available.

If you regularly use external drives for pictures and video, be sure your plan includes their backup as well.

108. Phone camera

Technology has been advancing at an incredible rate. I remember getting a digital camera that was eight megapixels thinking it was incredible. Today's cell phones now have better cameras than that!

In 2015, I took a trip to Eastern Europe and was not looking forward to carrying around my Nikon camera. It takes great photos, but it is big and bulky (and, quite frankly, I'm not such a great photographer that I really needed to have a special camera with me).

I made the decision that I would try only taking photos on my cell phone. It was incredible; the photos came out great, and I was able to walk around cities unencumbered.

For avid photographers, I would never suggest leaving your camera at home. But, for the rest of us, who enjoy the photos but don't want to lug a bulky camera, consider using your phone.

Before you go, make sure you have sufficient storage space for photos and videos. And, if you want to make sure nothing is lost, have the pictures on your phone automatically back up to the Cloud. This way, even if your phone gets lost, your photos will still be safe.

CHAPTER 17
Organization

It is better to own less than organize more.
—Joshua Becker

The first step in organizing your stuff is to sort through the clutter and decide what gets to stay. In today's consumer society, we often have so much more than we can ever use…of just about everything.

The clutter weighs us down and becomes a burden. This is true for both adults and kids. When we have less stuff and are able to create some open space, we enable our minds to think more clearly.

Bulletin boards and bookshelves are often overflowing, filled to capacity, and visually unappealing. Taking everything off, sorting and deciding on what is most important can make a huge difference.

If you have too many things you love, consider rotating items so that you actually see what you have.

When it comes to our kids, we often associate buying gifts with showing love. Next time you're tempted to do this, think about finding an experience to share with them instead. The memories are more meaningful than the objects. And they don't create clutter!

109. A place for everything

A place for everything and everything in its place.
—BENJAMIN FRANKLIN

This quote appears simple and yet we often have trouble putting it into practice. If we did, lost keys and wallets, misplaced phones, and missing documents would be a thing of the past.

The key to implementing this philosophy is creating systems that work for you. For example, a bowl for keys placed by the door you most often use to enter and exit your home, could create a useful habit for all family members.

A valet for men to put their wallet and watch on where they typically undress, enables them to empty pockets at the end of each day, knowing where these items will be each morning. And, perhaps most universal, is plugging your phone in to charge/backup each night in the same location.

If you put a new system in place, you will need to be disciplined about using the system for a few weeks. This will turn the action into routine.

Creating systems enables you to develop the habit and discipline of "a place for everything and everything in its place." This will ultimately save you time and aggravation that would otherwise be spent searching.

110. The two-minute rule

The two-minute rule is most often attributed to David Allen, author of *Getting Things Done: The Art of Stress-Free Productivity.*

Sometimes the smallest actions have the greatest impact. This is true about getting through so many of the small tasks that we are faced with each day.

Interestingly, polishing off a bunch of small, quickly done tasks can energize us and motivate us to handle the larger, more mentally taxing projects that need to get done.

This philosophy can be applied successfully at both work and home.

Work:

When you set aside time to sort through e-mails, identify those that simply require a short response. Using the two-minute rule, take care of the quick and easy e-mails and save the more thoughtful responses for later. It is also a quick task to delegate e-mails that need to be addressed by a colleague.

Word of caution:

Like anything, the two-minute rule should be used in moderation. It is not difficult to imagine spending an entire day completing small, two-minute tasks and never getting the real, challenging work done!

Home:

One of my favorite examples of the two-minute rule is getting into the habit of hanging up your coat.

I have a large family (six of us). Can you imagine what it would look like if everyone came in from outside and simply dropped his or her jacket on the kitchen floor? Even if they put their coats on the back of the kitchen chairs…What a mess!

Hanging your coat up, every time you come inside, is a habit that takes less than two minutes but makes your space look considerably better with very little effort.

This is especially true if you get your entire household on board!

There are many tasks that are time and labor intensive. But a lot of what we do each day can be done, and checked off the list, in under two minutes.

What falls into this category? Here are just a few things that come to mind in addition to hanging up your coat:

- Making your bed
- Some e-mail responses
- Responding to an invitation
- Entering information in your calendar
- Putting a task on your to-do list
- Putting dirty dishes in the dishwasher

Using the two-minute rule as a guide will save you time and help you be more productive.

111. Inboxes

A few years ago we all thought the world was rapidly moving toward a paperless society. Unfortunately, this has not yet happened; I'm not sure it ever will.

A traditional inbox whether in an office or a home, is a good place to catch the things that require your attention.

It is not, however, a good place for long-term storage. Inboxes need to be sorted through every day or two; otherwise items fall to the bottom and are forgotten.

There are two types of inboxes—digital and physical.

Digital inboxes are intended for e-mails. As we discussed early in this book, it helps to limit how often you process your e-mail. Sorting at regular intervals, instead of constantly, will save you time and reduce your stress.

Tasks embedded in e-mails need to be captured on your to-do list before being removed from your e-mail inbox. Once on a to-do list, the e-mail can go into a designated folder or one marked Processed.

This way, you can still access the e-mail if you need it as you are working on the task. Of course, some e-mails can simply be deleted or responded to right away.

Physical inboxes are useful for daily papers and snail mail. Like e-mails, it is better to select a time to go through your inbox rather than checking it constantly. Items in your inbox that are tasks need to go on your to-do list. If the paper stays in your inbox, you will likely look at it over and over again, each time you actively process the papers in the inbox.

You may want to consider filing the paper in the appropriate place and taking it out when you are ready to work on the task.

Like e-mails, many papers can be tossed or addressed immediately. This will help to reduce the volume of paper in your inbox.

If you have an inbox, it is important to check it frequently. Unlike your digital inbox, there is no alert or notification that pulls your attention to it. It's purely manual.

112. "File" is a four-letter word

You might hate filing; many people do. It can be tedious, boring, and the last thing you want to spend time on. But, until you are paperless, it is a necessary evil.

I know I am probably in the minority, but I enjoy filing (although the amount of paper I have has severely diminished in recent years). It creates a sense of order and with a good system, it means you can easily find things.

I always recommend that you file papers the same way you file e-mails and documents on your computer. Your system should be consistent. It will require less thought on your part, when you are looking for something (or filing it), and it makes it infinitely easier for coworkers or family members if they need to get something when you are unavailable.

I have been known to call my home and ask a kid to pull a paper out of my file drawer. It is never a problem because my files are color-coded by section and then in logical, alphabetical order.

The system I use for papers is the same system I use for electronic documents and e-mails.

I've heard some pushback that if I'm out of the office and anyone can find anything, I won't be indispensable. Your thought process, creativity, and problem solving should be your defining role…not how you organize your files.

I think most employees are expected to be able to file their documents (paper and digital) in a way that can be used by anyone so that the firm is not at risk if you are not at your desk.

113. File, don't pile

I approach filing the same way I approach mail. You may prefer to do these activities weekly, but understand that it will take you longer when you decide to do it.

Mail takes about five to ten minutes a day. If you wait until the weekend, it might cost you an hour of time.

The same is true of filing. My suggestion is to file constantly; a few minutes each day keeps your office orderly and you will not need to set aside a large chunk of time each week, which is likely to become a lower priority than a pressing issue.

Most importantly, a pile of papers is not a filing system. Remember—you should be protecting your firm. If you are out and nobody can find an important document (even if you know exactly where it is in the third pile from the left), you are affecting the firm in a negative way.

114. Clear desk = clear thinking

When you sit at your desk, what do you see? Is it an overstuffed bookcase? A bulletin board crammed with notes, invitations, and photos? A desktop with piles of papers, office supplies, and dusty photo frames?

When you are engaged in difficult tasks, what you are looking at matters. Our brains are engaging all of our senses all of the time. If what we see is a lot of clutter, it will make it more difficult than it needs to be to get hard work done.

There has recently been press about scientific evidence that shows that for innovative thinking, some noise and clutter helps stimulate creativity. If you feel that this is true for you, by all means borrow your colleague's cluttered office when you need to do this kind of work.

In general, an office that is organized, clean, and uncluttered will better serve you.

115. Photos on your phone

Almost every cell phone upgrade now includes higher definition photos and videos. I have finally reached the point that when I go on vacation, I don't bring a separate camera because it is so convenient to use my phone and the photo quality is great.

As you can imagine, my photos are extremely well organized. But a few years ago, I realized that I made a big mistake in my phone settings. I had accidentally shut off the geo-tagging feature on the camera. The geo-tagging feature automatically tags your photo with the location where it is taken. What a fantastic feature! Between this and the date and time stamp, all you need to do with your digital photos is tag the people in the picture.

If you have an iPhone, here are the simple steps to make sure your geo-tagging feature is on:

In Settings, click on Privacy and then Location Services.
Scroll down and click on Camera.
Allow Location access "While Using the App" (select this option.)
That's it!

116. Hang up your clothes

I don't want to sound like your mother, but I'm sure you've been told this before. Much like the two-minute rule, hanging up your clothes will keep your room tidier and save extra, unnecessary work later.

Kids are often guilty of putting clean clothes in the hamper because it's easier than hanging them up or folding them and putting them away. So the earlier you train them to put their clothes where they belong as they are coming off, the better.

Many adults are also guilty of not hanging up their clothes. Treadmills railings are often a favorite spot for tossing clothes—perhaps it is to reduce feelings of guilt associated with an unused piece of fitness equipment. After all, if it's holding clothes at least it has a legitimate purpose.

Much like getting into a made bed each night, having your clothes properly put away will make you feel better about being in your bedroom. Less clutter means less distraction and a better night's sleep.

It also means that if you wake up during the night you won't see scary shadows created by the clothes, which, for a moment, make you think there is an intruder in your room. (Has that ever happened to you?)

The only exception is the clothes you lay out to be worn the next day.

117. Create memory boxes

Hands down, this is my favorite tip for decluttering your home. While some individuals are not overly emotional about memorabilia, it's hard for most people to get rid of some of the cute pieces of art your now teenage child brought home from nursery school. Remember the little handprint that was made into a Thanksgiving turkey? Or perhaps it's your own college ID from thirty years ago.

These types of things have no place in your kitchen drawer. If you would like to hold onto memorabilia, create a memory box. (I suggest having one for each person in your home.)

The box does not need to be organized or neat—in fact, there is something fun about rummaging through a box of random items. But I do suggest that it be a clear plastic bin with a lid and not so large that you can't lift it when it's full. If you need a second box, it's fine—the clear plastic bins will stack nicely. Cardboard boxes tend to collapse when stacked and are also susceptible to rodents and moisture.

So what types of things can go in your memory box? For my kids, it includes their baby book, first shoes, select artwork, creative writing, favorite stuffed animal, HS varsity letters, etc. Mine includes report cards (my kids' are scanned but you could certainly put theirs in their memory box), autograph books from middle school and elementary school, creative writing, Red Cross swim cards, letters from summer camp, and all sorts of other fun items to look through.

When my kids were younger, they would sometimes have difficulty paring down what they put in the box. Each Thanksgiving morning, I would sit with them one at a time, and we would go through everything in their box. I could not get rid of something they wanted, and they could not get rid of something I thought they should keep. This worked incredibly well, and each year they got greater perspective on what they wanted to keep. It was an incredible life lesson on how to pick and choose what to hold onto and how to make some hard choices when you can't keep everything (the box had to close).

Having a specific place for memorabilia honors the memories without cluttering your home. When we are surrounded by clutter, it is difficult to be our most productive because we waste a lot of time searching through piles of meaningless items.

118. Declutter

> *The inside of a house or apartment after decluttering has much in common with a Shinto shrine…a place where there are no unnecessary things, and our thoughts become clear.*
> —MARIE KONDO

When we think about physical clutter, most of our stuff falls into the following categories:

1. Collections—will this be worth something?
2. Things we thought we would use, but don't
3. Sentimental memorabilia
4. Expensive items that were a luxury to buy
5. Things to have just in case we need it

Chances are many of these purchases are really mistakes that our brains have difficulty processing.

A recent study at Yale University identified that two areas in our brain that are associated with pain, light up in response to letting go of items we own and feel a connection toward. It is literally painful to let go of those things to which we have an emotional, physical, or financial attachment.

Being more discerning in our purchasing habits will result in owning fewer items. Having less means reducing the pain associated with discarding our unwanted clutter.

119. Invest in experiences

A 2010 Cornell University study by Travis J. Carter and Thomas Gilovich shows that experiences have greater value than material items.

After buying something we often experience negative emotions. We have buyer's remorse thinking that we might not have bought the right item at the best price. Whatever happiness is derived from a purchase diminishes over time.

Experiences (going to the theater, taking a vacation, or hiking for the afternoon) generate more positive, lasting emotions. Our satisfaction with experiences tends to increase over time.

Over the longer term, it is the experiences that generate happiness and satisfaction. Not the purchases.

Conclusion

Congratulations, you made it through 119 strategies that will help you to be Super-Productive!

If you've completed this book and are thinking that all these tips are fairly obvious and basic common sense, then I have done my job.

It should not be so hard to feel in control of your time so you can get the important things done and still have time to enjoy other things that make you happy.

I hope that you have started implementing some of the ideas and are already feeling less stressed and overwhelmed.

Would you like to receive more content? Visit my website, www. ControlChaos.org, and sign up for my blog. I'll be happy to send you my posts, which are published biweekly.

If you have found this book helpful, I would be truly grateful if you would leave a quick review on Amazon. Thanks!

120. Take action

The final strategy I can offer you is to take action. This is the key to making the most of this book. All you need is to create one small new habit at a time. When it becomes routine, you can add another and another.

Over time, you will find that the aggregate effect of these small changes is a significant change in your level of productivity and overall happiness and well-being.

Further Reading

The following is a list of the books, articles, studies, and videos referenced throughout the book.

Chapter I:

Kushlev, K., and Dunn, E. W. 2015. "Checking Email Less Frequently Reduces Stress." *Computers in Human Behavior* 43: 220–228. doi:10.1016/j.chb.2014.11.005

Chui, M, Manyika, J, Bughin, J, Dobbs, R, Roxburgh, C, Sarrazin, H, Sands, G, and Westergren, M. 2012. "The Social Economy: Unlocking Value and Productivity Through Social Technologies." McKinsey & Company, New York. Retrieved from http://www.mckinsey.com/industries/high-tech/our-insights/the-social-economy.

Linenberger, M. 2006. *Total Workday Control Using Microsoft Outlook: The Eight Best Practices of Task and E-Mail Management*. San Ramon: New Academy.

Chapter III:

Bluedorn, A. C., Turban, D. B., and Love, M. S. 1999. "The Effects of Stand-up and Sit-down Meeting Formats on Meeting Outcomes." *Journal of Applied Psychology* 84(2): 277–285. doi:10.1037//0021-9010.84.2.277

Retrieved from https://business.missouri.edu/publications/effects-stand-and-sit-down-meeting-formats-meeting-outcomes.

Chapter IV:

Sollisch, J. 2016. "The Cure for Decision Fatigue." *The Wall Street Journal.* Retrieved from http://www.wsj.com/articles/the-cure-for-decision-fatigue-1465596928.

Kleitman, N. 1982. "Basic Rest-Activity Cycle—22 Years Later." *Journal of Sleep Research & Sleep Medicine* 5(4): Retrieved from http://psycnet.apa.org/psycinfo/1983-22865-001.

Chapter V:

BBC. 2005. "UK | 'Infomania' Worse Than Marijuana." (April 22, 2005). Retrieved from http://news.bbc.co.uk/2/hi/uk_news/4471607.stm.

Achor, S. 2010. *The Happiness Advantage: The Seven Principles of Positive Psychology That Fuel Success And Performance At Work.* New York: Broadway Books.

Chapter VI:

Washington, Denzel. 2011. Penn's 2011 Commencement Address by Denzel Washington [Video File]. Retrieved from https://www.youtube.com/watch?v=vpW2sGlCtaE.

Konnikova, M. 2014. "The Struggles of a Psychologist Studying Self-Control." *NewYorker.com*. Retrieved from http://www.newyorker.com/science/maria-konnikova/struggles-psychologist-studying-self-control.

Chapter VII:

Kruse, K. 2015. *15 Secrets Successful People Know About Time Management: The Productivity Habits of 7 Billionaires, 13 Olympic Athletes, 29 Straight-A Students, and 239 Entrepreneurs.* Philadelphia: The Kruse Group.

Csikszentmihalyi, M. 1990. *Flow: The Psychology of Optimal Experience.* New York: Harper and Row.

Rhimes, S. 2016. My Year of Saying Yes to Everything [Video File] Retrieved from: https://www.ted.com/talks/shonda_rhimes_my_year_of_saying_yes_to_everything.

Chapter IX:

Schwartz, T. 2012. "More Vacation is the Secret Sauce." *HBR.org*. Retrieved from https://hbr.org/2012/09/more-vacation-is-the-secret-sa.

Perlow, L, and Porter, J. 2009. "Making Time Off Predictable—and Required." *HBR.com*. Retrieved from https://hbr.org/2009/10/making-time-off-predictable-and-required.

Kokalitcheva, K. 2015. "Early Morning is Actually the Worst Time to Drink Coffee." *Time.com*. Retrieved from http://time.com/3903826/coffee-early-morning-worst-time/

Neal, D, Wood, W, and Quinn, J. 2006. "Habits—A Repeat Performance." *Current Directions in Psychological Science*. Retrieved from https://www.researchgate.net/publication/252798940_Habits-A_Repeat_Performance.

Duhigg, C. 2012. *The Power of Habit: Why We Do What We Do In Life and Business*. New York: Random House.

McRaven, W. 2014. University of Texas Austin 2014 Commencement Address—Admiral William H. McRaven. [Video File] Retrieved from https://www.youtube.com/watch?v=pxBQLFLei70

Dutton, J. 2012. "Make Your Bed, Change Your Life?" *Psychology Today. com*. Retrieved from https://www.psychologytoday.com/blog/brain-candy/201208/make-your-bed-change-your-life.

Chapter X:

Gelles, D. 2015. "At Aetna, a C.E.O.'s Management by Mantra." *NYTimes.com*. Retrieved from https://nyti.ms/2kcJpYg.

McGonigal, K. 2012. *The Willpower Instinct: How Self-Control Works, Why It Matters, and What You Can Do to Get More of It*. New York: Avery.

Lazar, S. 2013. TEDX Cambridge Sara Lazar on How Meditation Can Reshape our Brains. [Video File] Retrieved from https://www.youtube.com/watch?v=H234h6wJ7LA.

Schulte, B. 2014. *Overwhelmed: How to Work, Love, and Play When No One Has the Time.* New York: Sarah Crichton Books, Farrar, Straus and Giroux.

Treasure, J. 2013. How to Speak so that People Want to Listen. [Video File] Retrieved from https://www.ted.com/talks/julian_treasure_how_to_speak_so_that_people_want_to_listen.

Chapter XI:

Achor, S. 2011. The Happy Secret to Better Work. [Video File] Retrieved from https://www.ted.com/talks/shawn_achor_the_happy_secret_to_better_work.

Kim, E., Hagan, K., Grodstein, F., DeMeo, D., De Vivo, I, and Kubzansky, L. 2016. "Optimism and Cause-Specifi Mortality: A Prospective Cohort Study." *American Journal of Epidemiology.* Retrieved from http://aje.oxfordjournals.org/content/early/2016/12/02/aje.kww182.short?rss=1.

Grant, A. M. 2014. *Give and Take: Why Helping Others Drives Our Success.* New York: Penguin Books.

Chapter XII:

Huffington, A. S. 2014. *Thrive: The Third Metric to Redefining Success and Creating a Life of Well-Being, Wisdom, and Wonder.* New York: Harmony Books.

Kahneman, D., Krueger, A., Schkade, D., Schwartz, N., and Stone, A. 2004. "A Survey Method for Characterizing Daily Life Experience: The Day Reconstruction Method." *Science.* Retrieved from http://science.sciencemag.org/content/306/5702/1776

Jones. J. 2013. In U.S., 40% Get Less Than Recommended Amount of Sleep. *Gallup.* Retrieved from http://www.gallup.com/poll/166553/less-recommended-amount-sleep.aspx.

Chapter XIII:

Duckworth, A. 2016. *Grit: The Power of Passion and Perseverance.* New York: Scribner.

Duckworth, A. 2013. Grit: The Power of Passion and Perseverance. [Video File] Retrieved from https://www.ted.com/talks/angela_lee_duckworth_grit_the_power_of_passion_and_perseverance.

Bregman, P. 2015. *Four Seconds: All the Time You Need to Stop Counter-Productive Habits and Get the Results You Want.* New York: HarperOne.

Chapter XVII:

Allen, D. 2001. *Getting Things Done: The Art of Stress-free Productivity.* New York: Viking.

Tolin, D., Kiehl, K., Worhunsky, P., Book, G., and Maltby, N. 2008. "An Exploratory Study of the Neural Mechanisms of decision-making in Compulsive Hoarding." *Psychological Medicine* 39(02): 325. doi:10.1017/s0033291708003371

Carter, T. J., and Gilovich, T. 2013. "Getting the Most for the Money: The Hedonic Return on Experiential and Material Purchases. *Consumption and Well-Being in the Material World,* 49–62. doi:10.1007/978-94-007-7368-4_3

Made in the USA
Middletown, DE
10 April 2017